PENGUIN BOOKS

HOW TO BECOME RIDICULOUSLY
WELL-READ IN ONE EVENING

Eric Oakley Parrott was born in 1924 in London, well within the sound of Bow Bells, and so was technically a Cockney, but was brought up in Shoreham-by-Sea, Sussex, where he attended the local grammar school. After winning that school's most coveted academic award, the Gregory Taylor Scholarship, in 1939, he went to Brighton Technical College, where he studied for a BSc in Mathematics and Geography. He then spent twenty years as a cartographer with the Hydrographic Department of the Ministry of Defence, and while there edited the Admiralty List of Radio Signals. He began to write seriously in his spare time – articles, plays and entries in various literary competitions. He always took a keen interest in the theatre and was both an amateur actor and a producer, becoming an Associate of the Drama Board in 1961. He had a number of his plays produced and his radio plays have been performed by the BBC and in Germany, Canada, Australia and New Zealand, among other countries. In 1976 he resigned from the Civil Service, and, after a year at Garnet College, Roehampton, taught English and general studies at Havering Technical College, Hornchurch, Essex. Here he compiled a number of Units for the Longman's General Studies Project. Failing eyesight forced him to retire from teaching and he then began a third career as a full-time writer. His books include *The Penguin Book of Limericks*, *Limerick Delight* (Puffin), *Imitations of Immortality*, *How to Become Absurdly Well-Informed About the Famous and the Infamous*, *The Dogsbody Papers*, *How to Be Tremendously Tuned In to Opera* and *How to be Well-Versed in Poetry*, all published by Penguin. Eric Oakley Parrott died in 1990.

How to Become Ridiculously Well-Read in One Evening

A Collection of Literary Encapsulations

Compiled and Edited by E. O. Parrott

Penguin Books

PENGUIN BOOKS

Published by the Penguin Group
Penguin Books Ltd, 27 Wrights Lane, London W8 5TZ, England
Penguin Putnam Inc., 375 Hudson Street, New York, New York 10014, USA
Penguin Books Australia Ltd, Ringwood, Victoria, Australia
Penguin Books Canada Ltd, 10 Alcorn Avenue, Toronto, Ontario, Canada M4V 3B2
Penguin Books (NZ) Ltd, 182–190 Wairau Road, Auckland 10, New Zealand

Penguin Books Ltd, Registered Offices: Harmondsworth, Middlesex, England

First published by Viking 1985
Published in Penguin Books 1986
20

For R.G.G.Price,
who taught me so much more than
how to recite Gray's 'Elegy in a
Country Churchyard'

INTRODUCTION

To be well-read is surely highly desirable. It is what those eminent historians who wrote *1066 And All That* would have called 'A Good Thing'. Yet there are so many pressing calls upon our leisure time nowadays that it has become harder and harder for many people to achieve this laudable ambition.

So, given the desire for a mind well-furnished with a knowledge of literature, what can be done? Should you refrain from *Crossroads* and *Coronation Street*, and forswear all panel games and quiz shows? Must you stop going to the local every night? Is it necessary to think the unthinkable and make the ultimate sacrifice of renouncing television altogether? Such a price is too high to pay, at least for anyone who still wishes to keep abreast of modern culture.

Fortunately, this book offers you a solution to the problem, for it contains some one hundred and fifty succinct and entertaining encapsulations of some of the best-known books in the English language, including a few foreign works familiar to us in translation. Through them you will rapidly acquire nearly all that is worth knowing about the books concerned without having to undergo the tedious necessity of reading even one of them.

Of course, the idea of abbreviated versions of highly respected works of literature is by no means new. Ever since Charles Lamb published his *Tales from Shakespeare*, many abridged or condensed versions of books have appeared. Not all were wholly admirable. Those of Dr Bowdler are, for instance, quite at variance with modern taste. It is now the fashion to seek for sexual meanings and pornographic undertones even in passages where almost certainly the author intended nothing of the kind.

Then again, there are those twist-by-twist summaries in crib-books produced to help people pass exams in English Literature. Although these all seem to have the praiseworthy intention of saving the student from having to read the original text, they are uniformly arid and boring, and why should one be forced to spend even one evening in such dull company? Boredom is now the only Deadly Sin; the more traditional Seven have come to be so much in line with modern thinking that they have been re-designated Virtues.

Although the eccentric few who have read the classics in the original texts tend to be rather scornful about such abbreviated versions, these latter do, in fact, have a wide currency. The BBC invariably makes drastic cuts in those books which it selects for serial reading, often reducing them to a quarter of their original length. Film and television companies are equally ruthless, often omitting considerable portions of the plot, or even quite major characters. You may recall that splendid film of *Hamlet* in which the audience was never informed that Rosencrantz and Guildenstern were alive, let alone dead. And there was not even a Fortinbras to sweep away the litter of dead bodies at the end. Even greater liberties are taken with the text when the classics are transferred to the garish world of the comic strip.

Literary encapsulations not only have respectability; they are ecologically desirable. If this one small book can replace one hundred and fifty much weightier tomes, acres and acres of virgin forest may receive a temporary reprieve from the axe, and be used instead to produce yet more copies of the *Sun*, or to provide more packets of biscuits with even more numerous and impenetrable layers of wrapping.

This book is very much in accord with present-day political and economic thinking about the Arts and Education. Those left-wing extremists who reacted with horror at the recent drastic cuts in money available for the purchase of books by public libraries and educational institutions will surely change their minds now that one volume can replace a whole shelf-full for most readers. They may argue that even greater cost-cutting is possible, thus saving much-needed public money for worthier items of expenditure, such as official cars, public functions, banquets, official visits abroad by councillors and MPs, not to mention Cruise missiles and warehouses in which to store EEC butter for posterity.

The way that this book was written may be of interest. When I was commissioned by Messrs 'Viking' to undertake its compilation, I wrote to some forty authors, many of them regular contributors to the weekly literary competitions in the *New Statesman* and the *Spectator*. I outlined the requirements, proposed a list of possible titles and then sat down to cope with the ensuing flood. There were only two rules: one referred to the limits on length, while the other laid it down that the summaries must be entertaining as well as enlightening. Any form could be employed – verse or prose, parody or pastiche, limerick or haiku, cautionary tale or letter – anything went so long as the desired result was achieved. Many contributors attempted up to forty titles, so that, in the end, I was forced to choose between ten versions of *Hamlet*, eight of *Macbeth* and so on. In a few cases, I have included more than one version of the same title, since some items were too good to be omitted.

Some manuscripts passed to and fro several times, amended, cut extensively or even totally rewritten, until both the author and I were satisfied that the end had been achieved without breach of the rules. Regrettably not all the good material that I received could be included. There was just too much of it, and a few items were, unhappily, too long. In short, the project became a literary competition extending over nearly twelve months, with the judge doing his damnedest to ensure that every entry was a prize-winner.

There have been many distinguished names in the ranks of literary competitors over the years: Walter De La Mare, Graham Greene, Frances Cornford, Arthur Marshall, Roger Woddis, Bernard Levin, Edward Blishen, Allan M. Laing, to name but a few at random. Both Sir John Betjeman's well-known poem *How to Get On in Society* and Henry Reed's parody of T.S.Eliot, *Chard Whitlow*, were originally entries in literary competitions. This book demonstrates, I think, that there are as many talented and witty writers among literary competitors as there ever were. It has been both a pleasure and a privilege to undertake the task of co-ordinating their efforts.

There have been a number of anthologies entirely devoted to selections from one literary competition or another, but this is the first time, I believe, that competitors have banded together to produce a whole book, nearly all of which is new, unpublished material. They all assure me that they have greatly enjoyed the project and the stimulus to creative activity which it provided. They give me the impression that they will not be satisfied until we begin another one. I hope I shall still be around to man the clearing-house and edit the results.

E.O.PARROTT

ANON:
Beowulf

Grisly old Grendel   gulped guys in his greed;
Beowulf bashed him   and boy! did he bleed!
Hoisted his hand up   and hung it on high –
So, dashed, he departed   now destined to die.

While Grendel all gory   lay gasping and glum,
Immersed in the mere   was his murderous Mum.
So soon as he snuffed it   she set out to slay
The heroes who, heartened,   were hitting the hay.

The king's chief companion   she crunched in her chops,
Bedewing the doormat   with deathly dark drops.
Then back to her bolt-hole,   on breakfasting bent,
She leaves the lone lords   this loss to lament.

But down to the depths   the dauntless one dives.
He splinters his sword   but surprise! he survives;
In the water's a weapon   the woman to whack;
With the blade he bisects her   and bounces right back.

It's home he must hasten   'mid hug and hurrah,
Having mopped up the menace   of monster and Ma;
But a weird Worm awaits him   and wealth for the warrior –
Though the sortie's successful   the slaughterer's sorrier.

For the pest with its powerful   poison has pricked him
And vitally vanquished   are victor and victim.
A funeral soon follows   with faggots enflamed,
And in deadliest detail   his deeds are declaimed.

How brave was this Beowulf   brilliant and bold,
Gaffed Grendel and Gammer   and gained the Worm's gold;
Let his lion-like exploits   be listed at length
For students whose stamina's   stout as his strength.

MARY HOLTBY

ANON:
Everyman

Yf thisen be onne of ye newe-fangeld playes, methinken I preffur Moriss dancynge. An olde bor, Everymanne, getteth a summons from Godde vya Dethe, that he muste mete Hisen Makir. Notte serprisyngelie, hisen frendes and relatyones refusen to goe withe hym, an nether wille his Beauty, Wits, an soe onne. Onlie a dul fellow, Knowledge and his Goode Deedes, wille venture withe hym through the Grave. Yt wasen here that methinken thys be naught butte a commersyal for ye Churche. After Confessione – sepryse, sepryse! – Everymanne ys received intoe Heavene by ane Angell.

Iffe thys be a Moralitie Playe, I wold preffere ane Imoralitie. Methynken thysen crase for plase will goe the way of Spellynge Reforme.

E.O.PARROTT

RICHARD ADAMS:
Watership Down

Frith knows, they'd come a long way.

As the evening leollim slanted across Watership Down, Hazel saw it all again in his mind's eye.

'Do you recall that fateful day back in the old warren, when you told us of the impending grargfaff?' he asked Fiver who was nerilting nearby.

'Oh yes, Hazel,' said Fiver. 'But the thought of the journey ahead gave me the thuttibns. We couldn't have done it without you.'

'But it was your drel-ngorks which warned us, Fiver.'

Fiver kiffed a stimbdm thoughtfully. 'I didn't know we would have to face so many karb-li-lerks, though,' he said. 'The quaquadders in the wood. The filldnus by that ominous brerk. Those awful obidthisses . . .'

'Oh yes, Fiver. Times have been hard. Do you remember the farm where I got trapped by the brarkims? And how glum we all became when we realized that without does there could be no plitts?'

'How could I forget? That frightening expedition to Efrafa to fetch some. When I think back I had the thuttibns most of the time.'

'Nonsense, Fiver,' barked Bigwig as he hopped over to them with his following of admiring youngsters. 'You're talking terlg. You were as blieophra as anyone on Watership Down.'

'But what about when General Woundwort attacked?' asked Fiver. 'I was chargg-scared then, you know.'

'We were all chargg-scared, Fiver,' Bigwig smiled. 'But we didn't give in. None of us. We gave old Woundwort a drerbubbing he'll never forget.' And he rolled over, proudly displaying his grofmpts to the awe-struck youngsters.

'I suppose we all had our prol to play,' laughed Hazel. 'Even Kehaar, though it was as much as I could do to make frick or tlebb of what he said. Those big white ullucks have a language all of their own.'

'A what?' queried Fiver.

'A language.'

'Do you mean the way they dtrnymn?'

'No. I told you. A language. It's what they use to communicate.'

'To what, Hazel?' asked Bigwig.

Hazel sighed and resumed nerilting. Frith knew, they had a long way to go.

N.J.WARBURTON

KINGSLEY AMIS:
Lucky Jim

Over the top goes lucky Jim:
Cheek is the gas that raises him.
Deep in the scrub of Academe,
Things are not always what they seem;
Jim can be found in funny places,
Making unprofitable faces,
Gulped at by girls, gagging in glees,
Sheets and boats burnt with equal ease,
Lost in his lecture, stoned and stuck –
One might assume his lack of luck.

Wide though the chasm, Jim will jump it,
Carry off kudos, cash and crumpet;
All who would sink while others swim
Fix their unlikely hopes in him –
Over the top goes lucky Jim.

MARY HOLTBY

JANE AUSTEN:
Emma

Miss Bates has a visitor:

'My dear Mrs Cole, how very kind – yes, quite well, I
thank you – do pray take a seat. We have such news! Have you heard –
No? Well, I think it is all a secret, so perhaps I should not say but no
one had any idea – except Jane and Mr Churchill, of course, and all
the time we thought he was only calling about my mother's spectacles.
Dear Jane is much better already – we are so thankful. Do oblige us
by taking some refreshment – one of Mr Knightley's baked apples –
some cake? Miss Woodhouse called yesterday and was so good as to
taste a small slice and pronounce it delicious – such kindness. She is
now out with Jane – she takes the news extremely well, considering –
no sign of disappointment – Box Hill, yes, delightful – but I am afraid
my silly chatter sometimes – however, Mr Churchill did seem so very
attentive – but then we are *all* so fond of the excellent Miss
Woodhouse – but to think all this time – one can hardly credit – it was
poor Mrs Churchill dying, you know, that let it all out. We have
surprises indeed in Highbury, do we not, Mrs Cole? First, Mr Elton
suddenly brings back a bride – charming – but some thought he
showed a marked preference for Miss Smith, some thought for
another – I never notice such things – and now on top of Jane being
engaged to Mr Churchill we hear Miss Smith is to marry the good
Mr Martin of Abbey Mill Farm – oh, must you be going? So sorry
you will not take a baked apple, one of Mr Knightley's – he will be
marrying next, I should not be surprised – so much talk of marrying
going on – and there's our dear Miss Woodhouse – what could be
more suitable?'

JOYCE JOHNSON

JANE AUSTEN:
Mansfield Park

From a family not all that canny,
Our poor little nine-year-old Fanny
    Is sent, all nonplussed,
    To a strange upper crust
Collection of cousins and aunts
Who do little her lot to enhance.

She learns what is *infra* (their) *dig* –
And grows up into rather a prig.
    But for Edmund's affection,
    She might, on reflection,
Have grown into a real problem kid,
But the Bertrams know naught of the id.

Fanny, duly subdued, 'knows her place',
So much so, that, when called on to face
    A social assembly,
    She goes all over trembly,
And performance, unless she can feel
Unobserved, is a painful ordeal.

The Miss Bertrams – there's little denied them
Except principles given to guide them –
    Live unenviable lives
    When they both become wives;
But Fanny's as happy as Larry,
For Edmund and she at last marry.

It is clear that an indolent ma
And a stern and formidable pa,
    Plus a flattering aunt
    Who indulges them, can't
Be good for young elegant daughters,
No matter how stately their quarters.

JOYCE JOHNSON

JANE AUSTEN:
Persuasion

How barren is the baronet
    Who in production falters,
So far as only girls to get! –
    This fate was poor Sir Walter's.
An Elliot of the purest breed,
    His rank he strongly fancies,
But Kellynch Hall he must concede
    Because of strained finances.
His tenant is a naval man
    And, curiously, related
To one who'd wooed his daughter, Anne,
    Which she'd reciprocated.
Eight years ago this gentle soul
    To chuck him was persuaded,
By friends and kin, though, on the whole,
    She could not think as they did.
Back in her life (a trifle stiff),
    He flirts with pert Louisa,
Who likes to take the high-jump if
    His hands are there to seize her.
But once too often, tempting fate,
    This miss just missed her mister,
Who carried her inanimate
    To those who could assist her.
She from her fall – and Frederick –
    Conveniently recovers,
And both are commendably quick
    To gather other lovers.
(Sir Walter's heir supports the trend:
    Of Anne profanely dreaming,
He swaps her for her father's friend –
    An end to mutual scheming.)
For Fred at heart's a faithful man
    And early takes occasion
Once more to speak his love to Anne,
    Who now needs no *Persuasion*.

MARY HOLTBY

... in One Evening

JANE AUSTEN:
Pride and Prejudice

'Marry well' is Bennet tenet: Bingley singly must remain
Since classy Darcy (Lizzy-dizzy) thinks he's far too good for Jane.
Rummy mummy, jaunty aunty, these would drag both gallants down –
Plus the younger siblings' dribblings over officers in town.
See the specious Wickham trick 'em with his tales of birthright gloom,
See how hideous Lydia's ruin looms before she gets her groom;
Glassy Darcy saves the bacon, shaken out of former pride:
Is he Lizzy's destined love, to shove her prejudice aside?
Has she clout to flout that matron, patroness of priestly coz
(He whose ludicrous proposing Rosings rules – like all he does)?
Darcy oughter court her daughter, destined his through two
    decades . . .
'Mulish, foolish girl, remember Pemberley's polluted shades!'
Dare she share his great estate, or can't Aunt Catherine be defied?
Yes! and ere their bells ring jingly, Bingley too shall claim his bride.

MARY HOLTBY

JANE AUSTEN:
Sense and Sensibility

This is the tale of Marianne,
Who fell in love with one young man,
So handsome, witty, warm and strong,
She thought that he could do no wrong.
Thus, when he went away and wed
An heiress who was rich, instead,
It ruined all her dreams romantic,
And drove the poor girl nearly frantic.
She carried on, and would not smile
Upon a colonel, who the while
Had loved her with a strong affection.
What this girl wanted was Perfection,
But he spoke no impassion'd verse,
He seemed so old – and what was worse –
He wore a flannel waistcoat.

Her sister, who had much more sense,
Although her feelings were intense
When *she* felt left upon the shelf,
Had kept them strictly to herself.
Meanwhile she cared for Marianne,
And in due course the girl began
To see the imbecility
Of over-sensibility.
Her sister, too, got back her man,
And much rejoiced when Marianne
Began to look upon the colonel
With feelings more than just fraternal,
For she had known, right from the start,
That there can beat a constant heart
Beneath a flannel waistcoat.

JOYCE JOHNSON

SAMUEL BECKETT:
Waiting for Godot

The lesson is taken from the gospel according to Beckett, Acts I and II.

ACT I.

1 And there were in that place two men abiding by a tree waiting for Godot. And the first was called Vladimir and the other was called Estragon.

2 And Estragon wrestled with his boot for to remove it. But he could not.

3 And Vladimir was sore troubled by the weakness of his bladder and departed from that place many times and tarried a little way off to relieve himself.

4 Then appeared unto Vladimir and Estragon a master and his servant who was heavy laden and had a rope about his neck. And the master's name was Pozzo and the servant's name was Lucky.

5 And they spake of many things and departed.

6 Then did a young boy appear and spake unto Vladimir and Estragon saying, Godot will not be with you this day. He will come unto you on the morrow. And the young boy departed.

7 And the evening and the morning were another day.

ACT II.

1 And lo, the tree blossomed and shot forth leaves. And Vladimir and Estragon saw that it blossomed.

2 And while they tarried beneath that tree they spake many things.

3 And behold, Pozzo and Lucky came unto them again. And the sight of Pozzo was taken away and the voice of Lucky was struck dumb.

4 And when they had gone there appeared unto them again a young boy.

5 And Vladimir and Estragon said to the boy, Go, tell Godot that we are here, that you have seen us with your own eyes.

6 Then did they become angry with the young boy who departed from that place with great haste.

7 And oft-times did Vladimir and Estragon wish in their hearts for death to embrace them. But the way of such deliverance was not at hand.

8 And it came to pass that nothing else came to pass.

V. ERNEST COX

MALCOLM BRADBURY:
The History Man

When a Marxist *poseur*, Howard Kirk –
Who, though smart, is a bit of a jerk –
    A trifle imprudently
    Screws a young student, she
Gets alpha-plus for her work.

For a priggish and solemn young Tory,
Alas, it's a different story.
    He complains to the prof,
    Who warns Howard off
In a way ineffectual and hoary.

For Howard enjoys confrontation!
He also attempts a flirtation
    With a dourish young Scot,
    Who appears to be not
Quite his type, being pro-education.

The revolting young students back Howard,
Because he's not ivory-towered;
    For averting their sit-in,
    Which he's done his bit in
Promoting, with plaudits he's showered.

The moral of this? Sad to say,
Machiavellianism *does* pay.
    Though a bullying coward,
    The rebarbative Howard
Screws the Scot, keeps his job, wins the day!

PETER NORMAN

CHARLOTTE BRONTË:
Jane Eyre

Orphan Jane is both plain and unhappy,
Her guardian has favourites, is snappy;
    This pious old ghoul
    Sends her ward off to school,
Hoping Lowood will make her less yappy.

Thinly clothed, poorly fed, badly taught,
Jane despairs as her plans come to naught,
    Till she's offered a job
    With an upper-class yob,
Who is brooding, erotic and fraught.

Jane leaves when the boss gets too randy
(He's still got a wife – ain't that dandy?);
    Then Fate plays a hand –
    Jane is left twenty grand,
Which for Jane (and the plot) is quite handy.

Back at Thornfield the lad's less erratic
Since Bertha's escape from the attic;
    Jane hears of the arson,
    Then sends for the parson,
And Rochester's blindly ecstatic.

TIM HOPKINS

EMILY BRONTË:
Wuthering Heights

Kilroy Hall,
Ballymuddle,
Ireland

19th December, 1848.

Mr Ellis Bell.

Sir,

Begging your indulgence and dependent on your publisher's assistance, I am driven to tell you of the revelation that has come with the reading of your literary opus 'WUTHERING HEIGHTS'.

Briefly, I am an elderly orphan whose life's work has been to search for the father I never knew. My existence (although comfortably endowed by the great wealth of my mother's family) has been impoverished by this man's absence. This man – dare I say it, Sir? – who lives and breathes in the very character and fortune of 'Heathcliff'; and, understanding that an author is best served by writing from experience, I believe I dare – my pen trembles in my hand – to call you, Sir, FATHER!

It is all there in the beginning of your book – his story, as I heard it at my mother's knee: the boy, brought from Liverpool, like a stray dog, to the sombre house; the glooming moors; the hostile son-of-the-house; the mercurial daughter. The rivening passions driving him away to seek a gentler landscape and people. The significance in the name of the good servant, Nellie Dean – my father used to sing a song which told of her.

Had my mother lived longer, I might have garnered some clues as to why my father left her as he did; and there's the ever-burning question: would he – you – have stayed had he known she was with child?

Mr Bell (a pseudonym, no doubt), your story tells me what I should have suspected, that great need would draw you inexorably back to Yorkshire. A passion such as that for Cathy I can understand, but I am deeply disappointed in the marriage to such as Isabella Linton and wonder if it was, in fact, bigamous? There is so much that I would like to discuss with you.

Dare I hope we can, at last, meet face to face? Failing this, perhaps you would, at least, return the gold and jewellery that disappeared (from my mother's strong-box, if you remember) on the same day that you did.

Hopefully,

Clifford Heath

BRENDA WHINCUP

JOHN BUNYAN:
A Pilgrim's Progress

Celestial City
Tuesday

Found a fantastic place to stay, but had one helluva journey getting here! Very despondent first day when I got stuck in a bog at Slough. Luckily Help was at hand. Met worldly wise fellow from Carnal Policy (bit like Milton Keynes), who misdirected me. Prat! An evangelist chappie set me back on the straight and narrow, and I reached the Cross where I lost all my luggage! Still, it's an ill wind – walking was much easier with nothing to carry!

Got my visa for Celestial City and lost the damn thing! Had to go back and find it. Stayed a couple of nights at Beautiful House run by some very nice people. Place was full of books and antiques – Moses's rod, David's sling, etc. When I left they gave me a suit of armour which fitted a treat.

Attempted mugging by weirdo in Valley of Humiliation, but fought him off. Then into Valley of Shadow of Death – really spooky! Got through and joined up with Faithful companion. Called at Vanity Fair (worse than Petticoat Lane) and was beaten up and thrown into clink. Tried by Lord Hate-Good – my mate was executed by burning! I was remanded but managed to escape.

Met Hopeful (you'd like him), who came all the rest of the way. Some nutter caught us trespassing in Doubting Castle, duffed us up and locked us in dungeon. Remembered I had master key, and we got out.

Things started looking up a bit after that. Delectable Mountains were super. Lovely views. Spent night with nice old shepherds. Eventually got to Beulah. Weather was fantastic. Struggled across river – nearly drowned, but my pal Hopeful saved me!

Finally arrived at Celestial City – God, what a fabulous reception! After all I've been through, this is absolute heaven!

Wish you were here.

All the best,

Christian

V. ERNEST COX

ANTHONY BURGESS:
A Clockwork Orange

Young Alex breaks people like toys;
He's cured by a course which destroys
    His freedom of will;
    Relapses until
He grows up and . . . boys will be boys.

CLAUDIO VITA-FINZI

SAMUEL BUTLER:
The Way of All Flesh

In a vicarage, Ernest was born,
Where, upon him, quite soon, it would dawn
    That his ma was a sneak,
    And his pa was un-meek,
And he'd have to learn Greek, night and morn!

Then, at 'Varsity, he became sure
That a life free from sin would endure;
    So before his zeal waned,
    He was quickly ordained,
To become a young curate – still pure!

Till one day, rash Rev. Pontifex thought
He'd try sex – whether gratis, or bought;
    With a conscience quite frayed,
    He attacked a shy maid –
And got six months in quod, for that tort!

Then he thinks he should marry – and save –
A young bint, for whose favours men crave;
    But she doesn't repent,
    And soon spends ev'ry cent
On pink gin, while poor Ernest must slave!

Soon he learns his aunt's left him her dough,
And his marriage is bigamous: so,
    He calls: 'Thank-You, up there!',
    Puts the children in care,
And retires to write books ... Novels? ... No!!

PASCO POLGLAZE

LEWIS CARROLL:
Alice in Wonderland

'You are young, Alice dear,' it was Elsie who spoke,
    'You are truthful, and nice and polite,
But such nonsense you've talked ever since you awoke –
    Are you sure you are feeling all right?'

'In my dream,' replied Alice, 'I often felt queer;
　　I was either too big or too small.
It is quite a relief to find, now that I'm here,
　　I'm the right size again, after all.'

'You are young,' Elsie said, 'yet you used to recite
　　Without making a single mistake,
But the rhymes you've repeated are plainly not right.
　　Have you any excuse, dear, to make?'

'In my dream,' she replied, 'nothing came as I meant,
　　And even the Mock Turtle's song –
Like the words of my *How doth the little* – all went
　　So dreadfully, stupidly wrong.'

'You are young, Alice dear, yet you seem to have been
　　Meeting grown-ups and able to chat
With all kinds of people, including a Queen,
　　What made you feel equal to that?'

'In my dream,' replied Alice, 'they argued without
　　Any sensible reason whatever.
Any sense in their nonsense I never made out;
　　By comparison, I felt quite clever.'

'You are tired,' said Elsie. 'It's time, too, for bed.
　　Just tell me the end of your dream.
I was brushing some leaves off, away from your face,
　　When you woke with an odd little scream.'

'In my dream,' replied Alice, 'the Queen of Hearts had
　　Just shouted out "Off with her head!",
And then I woke up, I was really quite glad.
　　Was it you saying "Off now to bed!"?'

JOYCE JOHNSON

LEWIS CARROLL:
Through the Looking-Glass

Alice, still thinking of the White Knight's song, tells her sister a little of what she found there.

'I'll tell thee briefly as I can,
    But there's so much to say.
A game of chess – that was the plan,
    And I a pawn in play.
The Red Queen told me quite a lot
    And who it was I'd meet;
To keep us in the self-same spot,
    She ran me off my feet!

'I wish you could have seen them all –
    Two fat boys dressed for fight;
And Humpty Dumpty on his wall;
    The curious White Knight
With oddest things upon his horse,
    All of his own invention.
Then I became a Queen, of course,
    As had been the intention.

'And now, if late for tea or bed,
    (To close this little rhyme),
I think of what the Red Queen said
    And curtsey to save time,
And laugh, for it reminds me so
Of characters I came to know –
The twins who led me off to show
The Red King and his dream, although
I'm not just part of it – oh no!
And then the black and monstrous crow,
The White Queen crying, "Oh, oh, oh!"
Before she hurt her finger so,
The sheep who told me how to row,
The White Knight, sad and kind and slow,

That time the Looking-Glass, like snow,
Melted in mist, and let me go
        Through to the other side.'

JOYCE JOHNSON

MIGUEL DE CERVANTES:
Don Quixote

A sort of knightly Mr Fix-it,
That's the story of Don Quixote,
Who travelled, battled, all in vain,
And then returned to fight again.

Sancho Panza, sort of minder,
Monkey to the organ-grinder,
Watched the exploits of his chief,
And rubbed his eyes in disbelief
To see him fight a flock of ewes,
Or, in his dottiness, confuse
Some windmills with a hostile army,
Though slow, he saw his boss was barmy.

Sexploits? Picture Don Juan
Making love like Peter Pan.
That's as near as Dulcinea
Came to getting into gear.
Our Don thought a lot of her:
But that was all – just thought of her.

What made the man the more absurd
Was that he often could be heard
Muttering in accents throaty:
'Am I really Don Quixote?'

W.S.BROWNLIE

RAYMOND CHANDLER:
The Big Sleep

My name's Philip Marlowe, the chivalrous shamus.
I'm not very rich and I'm not very famous.
For twenty-five dollars a day and expenses,
I move in a sub-world of thieves, pimps and fences.
Now General Sternwood has just had a feeler
From Arthur Gwynn Geiger, the fag porno dealer.
It seems that young Carmen, the General's daughter,
Has run up some debts and this Geiger had bought a
Fat sheaf of her I O Us, hoping to blackmail
Old Sternwood, for whom I'm a hot-on-the-track male.
Still other complexities thicken the mystery,
All somehow connected with family history:
Like where's Rusty Regan? (The vanishing Paddy
Who's missed by the Sternwoods, and not only Daddy,
But also by Vivian, Carmen's big sister,
Since he was her husband – a hell of a twister!)
So the plot is bizarre, hence my *précis* is minimal,
But it focuses on a degenerate criminal:
This guy Eddie Mars, and his web of ill-doing,
That accounts for a lot of the conflicts ensuing.
And the corpses pile up, but the principal five are
The smut-pedlar, Geiger; a horny young driver,
Who worked for the Sternwoods; Joe Brody, a vicious
Small-timer, who got his for being ambitious;
A P.I. called Harry Jones, sent into limbo
(The poor sap had fallen for Brody's ex-bimbo)
By Mars' man Canino – remorseless, inhuman –
Whom I shot myself to ensure the denouement.
Plus it turns out that Regan's as dead as a gopher,
But I'm damned if I figured who murdered the chauffeur.

BASIL RANSOME-DAVIES

RAYMOND CHANDLER:
Farewell, My Lovely

'I ran into this guy outside a dive.
I gathered that his name was Moose Malloy.
He didn't measure more than nine by five.
He picked me up as though I were a toy.

'He had a temper and he had a gun.
He shot the dude who ran the joint stone dead.
He only wanted to locate someone –
His darling little Velma, so he said.

'Moose amscrayed, but the case was getting hot.
I formed the picture, piece by dirty piece,
From Amthor, Mrs Grayle and Marriott
And Anne Riordan and the local police.

'It wasn't pretty, but they never are.
The *femme fatale* involved was Mrs Grayle.
Poor Moose had hitched his wagon to her star.
Like Lancelot, he couldn't help but fail.

'So what's it prove? That men are always fools,
And fall for gorgeous dames who cheat and lie,
And use their paramours as willing tools.
I'm glad I'm married to a fifth of rye.'

                                    BASIL RANSOME-DAVIES

RAYMOND CHANDLER:
The Long Goodbye

'When a pal's in a jam and he goes on the lam,
You've got to do something about it.
But is he really dead with a slug in his head
Down in Mexico? Frankly, I doubt it.

'Still, there's no time for thought when the action is taut,
And the life of a sleuth's never boring,
What with guarding a hack and the Verringer quack,
And the succulent, blonde Linda Loring.

'It's a hell of a deal, but a man doesn't squeal
When he's strictly a Bay City pro,
And the answer, I guess, like a problem in chess,
Just depends on the gambits you know.

'So I shrug and grimace, and I get on the case,
While the neighbourhood counts up its dead,
Till I've checked and outplayed the corrupt Mrs Wade –
And for once Marlowe makes it in bed.

'At the end of it all comes a dead-of-night call,
And it's Terry, my hollow-man friend,
And the treachery cuts like a knife in the guts,
And the shadows of *Weltschmerz* descend.'

BASIL RANSOME-DAVIES

GEOFFREY CHAUCER:
The Canterbury Tales

Some pilgrims to Caunterbury ryde,
(The host of the Tabard was gyde),
    Ful twenty and nyne
    From the Prioresse fyn
To the Wyfe of Bathe – fair, reed and wyd.

Every wight telle moste his tale,
And som were biyonde the pale
    With pilgrims on wyn,
    And Ypocras fyn,
Or ydronke on pleyn Southwerk ale.

Som tales were in prose, som in vers,
They were noble, mery or wers;
    The best telles of beestes,
    (The Nonne Preestes),
The Persones is a peyne in the ers.

FIONA PITT-KETHLEY

GEOFFREY CHAUCER:
The Man of Law's Tale

Poor Constance couldn't help inspiring lust,
Although she much preferred to preach and pray.
Good men and bad desired her fit to bust,
And jealous mothers made her sail away.
She had a rough time but I'm glad to say,
Since God was very firmly on her side,
The goodies triumphed and the baddies died.

WENDY COPE

GEOFFREY CHAUCER:
The Miller's Tale

Young Allie was a housewife
Who lived in Oxford Town,
And the lodger and the cleric longed
To take her knickers down.

Her husband, John, was thicker
Than the planks he worked by day,
And Nick the lodger worked a scheme
To have his wicked way.

He got old John to fearing
There'd be a second Flood,
That if he didn't get three tubs,
They'd all be drinking mud.

They got the tubs and climbed inside,
Old John fell fast asleep.
The lovers crept into his bed
And left him counting sheep.

Then came the love-sick cleric
To their window – what a farce!
'A kiss!' he pleaded. Allie scoffed:
'Here – kiss my bloody arse!'

The cleric fled, but promptly
With red-hot plough returned,
But now 'twas Nick who flashed his bum –
He got severely burned.

Aroused by cries for water
John howled: 'The Flood is here!'
The neighbours laughed: 'You're off your head!'
And Nicky nursed his rear.

RON RUBIN

ANTON CHEKHOV:
The Cherry Orchard

Dear Mr Lopakhin,

I understand you are well acquainted with Madam Ranyevskaia who arrived back from Paris recently with her younger daughter. Her brother ordered a waiting-room fire, flowers and refreshments. A billiard table was also provided, but this somewhat eccentric gentleman said that he preferred to play without one.

Unfortunately, the gentleman was not sufficiently eccentric to arrange for payment, and I am accordingly sending the account to you. I also enclose a bill for our samovar which the German governess made disappear in one of her conjuring tricks. It has not been seen since.

Your obedient servant,

Ivor Troika,

Station Master

Mr Lopakhin,

I beg to submit my account for a survey of the Ranyevsky family's orchard, preparatory to its redevelopment for holiday chalets. As I understood matters, my remuneration by Madam Ranyevskaia was in the nature of a wayward gift, and not a fee paid on your behalf. It was very disconcerting to be taken for a tramp, and, had I not previously assured you that I would not acknowledge you at that time, I should have protested.

I have heard rumours that you may be marrying the elder (adopted) daughter of that household. I beg to offer my premature good wishes.

With respect,

I. Choppitov,

Tree Surgeon

Mr Lopakhin,

I submit for your payment an account for a number of revolutionary tracts and leaflets supplied to Mr Trofimov who was living with the Ranyevsky family. I feel you would not wish it known that the younger daughter was studying inflammatory literature.

Yours truly,

V. Runnitov,

Printer & Bookseller

Dear Mr Lopakhin,

I had the honour to bring my little orchestra to play at Madam Ranyevskaia's house the night you bought the estate at the auction. May I offer my congratulations and my account for the evening's entertainment, as I understand that the lady in question has now returned to Paris at the request of an invalid gentleman friend?

I was sorry that Miss Varia took the news so badly. I think you did very wisely in not marrying into such a family. It does not do to marry girls who throw things, as I know very well.

Yours faithfully,

C. Klarinetsky

Dear Mr Lopakhin,

You may recall my daughter, Dooniasha, when she was a maid at the Ranyevsky residence. I am anxious to trace a certain Yasha, who is still with her former mistress in Paris as her valet. He is, I fear, no better morally than his mistress; my Dooniasha wonders if you would be kind enough to be her child's godfather.

Your obedient servant,

U. Nokitov

Dear Mr Lopakhin,

I enclose herewith my account for the cutting down of your orchard and demolition work on the adjoining house. Perhaps you would also let me have your instructions regarding the disposal of the body of the elderly ex-serf found on the premises.

With respect,

I. Choppitov,

Tree Surgeon

Dear Mr Lopakhin,

Please find herewith bill for signwork: One notice with inscription: 'Logs for Sale'.

S. Slapitonovitch,

Signwriter

E.O.PARROTT

ANTON CHEKHOV:
The Three Sisters

The doctor, Chebutykin, now ninety-seven, stands on the desolate platform of a station not a million miles from Moscow: he is marginally less drunk than he has been for over eighty years.

'Moscow – at last! I've come to see them off – but where are they? Still running after love, I suppose – that will o' the wisp. This Colonel Vershinin now – charming fellow, no doubt about that. But he doesn't love his wife – she's always too busy committing suicide. He loves Masha and Masha loves him. Masha doesn't love her husband – how could she? He's a fool. Then there's Irena, bored to distraction, loved by the Baron – until Soliony shot him, poor chap. What for? Because Soliony also loved Irena. But she didn't really care a kopek for either of them. And then there's Olga – a headmistress and hating it. And Andrey, their brother – fat and forty, tied to a shrew who's having an affair with the chairman of the local council. None of them happy, none of them fulfilled. And I, who loved their mother so hopelessly, so desperately, am I happy, am I fulfilled?'
[*Enter Anfisa's great-granddaughter.*]

'There you are, Ivan Romanych – we were hunting all over. Come home and rest now.'

'But they're going to Moscow.'

'Not today, lovey.' [*Aside*.] 'He forgets. They did all get to Moscow in the end and detested every minute of it.'

'Not going to Moscow?'

'Not from here anyway. They tore the rails up ages ago. It's all air packages to Yalta now.'

[*Chebutykin sighs and withdraws a bottle from his pocket*]

'Tarara-boom-di-ay, we're sitting on a bomb-di-ay.'

MARTIN FAGG

WILKIE COLLINS:
The Woman in White

Walter, a painter, returning one night,
Was suddenly met by a woman in white,
Escaped from a madhouse; she'd been put inside
For knowing the past of Sir Percival Glyde.

And then he met Marian, plain, with moustache,
And her young sister, Laura, who lacked her *panache*,
For, lovely and rich, she became the sad bride
Of debt-ridden, wicked Sir Percival Glyde.

Count Fosco then joined them in Blackwater Park;
He was fond of white mice, but his background was dark;
To share Laura's wealth he constantly sighed,
And hatched a foul plot with Sir Percival Glyde.

There were sudden departures and journeys by night,
And Laura was switched for the Woman in White.
The latter then very conveniently died,
And was buried as 'Wife of Sir Percival Glyde'.

Walter and Marian worked day and night
To prove Laura *wasn't* the Woman in White.
Sir Percival burned down a church on the side,
And proved he was neither a Sir nor a Glyde.

Count Fosco was slain by the Mafia – alas!
Ending up on a slab in the morgue behind glass.
Walter gained his reward with fair Laura as bride –
She'd grown sane at the death of Sir Percival Glyde.

O. BANFIELD

JOSEPH CONRAD:
Lord Jim

Lord Jim, the strong and silent sort,
And keen to do as Good Men ought,
Once lost his nerve and let things slip,
Abandoning a sinking ship,
Which, adding somewhat to the crime,
Was full of people at the time.
Though Fortune saved them from the drink,
The business made Jim's spirits sink.
Thus, since he was a decent chap,
He took himself right off the map;
So far, in fact, from White Men's eyes
It took a team of quite some size,
Narrating by both day and night,
To keep in touch with Lord Jim's plight.
Here he stayed, well under wraps,
And brooded on his moral lapse.
The locals hailed him as their lord,
Which, Jim felt, emphasized the fraud.
Then Fate took pity on the lad
By throwing up a thorough cad,
An evil Rotter, Brown by name,
Who helped Lord Jim wipe out his shame.
This villain's lust for spoil and strife
Gave Jim the chance to risk his life,
And undertake, much to his pride,
An act of Noble Suicide.

N.J.WARBURTON

JOSEPH CONRAD:
The Nigger of the *Narcissus*

The crew of the sail-ship *Narcissus*,
Of the nigger, James Wait, are suspicious;
    Is he swinging the lead –
    Or practically dead?
His effect on them all is pernicious.

Round the Cape they run into a storm,
'Tis a good job the Captain's on form;
    With stiff upper lip,
    He saves crew and ship,
While the nigger's laid up in his dorm.

Now it's James Wait's turn to sink –
He dies – and is dropped in the drink,
    One more week on the foam,
    Then that's it – the crew's home.
A bit short on laughs, don't you think?

V. ERNEST COX

DANIEL DEFOE:
The Fortunes and Misfortunes of the Famous Moll Flanders

Moll is a waif, whose mum's been transported,
But lucky for Molly, she's amply supported;

The good Mayor of Colchester sees to her cares,
But soon she's seduced, wed and having affairs.

She visits Virginia and finds her old mother,
Who tells her (Shock! Horror!) she's married her brother.

Shattered, she leaves him and sails homeward, grieving.
Skint, turns to crime, makes a bomb out of thieving.

Like mother like daughter, she's nicked pretty soon,
And shipped to Virginia, to a convicts' commune.

One of her ex-es turns up on the ship –
A highwayman (not just aboard for the trip).

They pool their resources, their ill-gotten gains,
And set up as planters (his brawn and her brains).

Mother pegs out and leaves Moll a plantation,
Which prospers (the profits are free from taxation).

Moll and her paramour reach their old age,
Rich and repentant, and terribly sage.

RON RUBIN

DANIEL DEFOE:
The Fortunes and Misfortunes of the Famous Moll Flanders

Moll Flanders – a girl of the street –
Was well-versed in the art of deceit;
    Transported for crime,
    Moll repents in good time.
She's the felon who fell on her feet.

V. ERNEST COX

DANIEL DEFOE:
The Life and Strange Surprising Adventures of Robinson Crusoe

Robinson Crusoe is wrecked on an isle;
Reckons he's going to be there for a while.

Saves some utensils and stores from the ship;
Builds a nice pad, somewhere comfy to kip.

Gadgets he makes and domesticates goats,
And scans the horizon each morning for boats.

He's years on his own till some cannibals call;
Crusoe saves one from a hell of a brawl;

Dubs him Man Friday; they get along fine;
Teaches him English and Matters Divine.

Time passes slowly, and then one fine day
Along comes a ship from the good old UK.

The captain is cursed with a mutinous crew,
But he sorts them all out without further ado.

Crusoe and Friday both thank the Almighty,
As the ship sets its course back home to old Blighty.

They finally reach what's called civilization,
But it's not known if Friday got through Immigration.

RON RUBIN

THOMAS DE QUINCEY:
Confessions of an English Opium Eater

I remember, I remember, it was in the bleak November,
When I started a flirtation with the Demon Opium.
I'd been suffering from headaches and some sympathetic
    medics
Recommended something stronger than my usual tot of
    rum.

Very soon I was addicted (as my friends had *not* predicted!),
Courteous reader, pain no longer pierced the region round
    my ears.
Intermittent aches had vanished, all anxieties were
    banished,
This euphoria continued: I knew peace for many years.

Then there came an alteration to this pleasant situation,
When the drug's avenging horrors started off to take their
  toll.
Frightful nightmares, for example, constituted but a sample
Of an Iliad of woes affecting body, mind and soul.

Farewell then, for ever after, happiness and jest and
  laughter;
Enter intellectual torpor, monster-haunted dreams and
  pain.
Pulsing, writhing, palpitating mental torment, indicating
The destruction of the body's finest faculty, the brain.

*Hopheads, junkies, double-dippers, snorters, fixers, main-line
  trippers,
Those who powderpuff their noses from the inside not the out;
Snow White and her Seven Giants, Mister Tambourine Man's
  clients,
Lucy in the Sky with Diamonds –
  THAT IS WHAT IT'S ALL ABOUT!*

T.L.McCARTHY

CHARLES DICKENS:
Bleak House

As a single-minded mouse
Gnaws the fabric of a house,
So the lawyers, gross and gray,
Eat the living world away.
That's *Bleak House*; but has it not,
Do I hear you say, a plot?
Yes, it has. This rambling book
Has characters like Guppy, Krook,
Ruthless Mrs Jellyby,
Model of philanthropy,
Harold Skimpole, child at heart,
Playing out his selfish part,
Pious Chadband and Miss Flite,
Far too many to recite,

Penniless, pretentious, fey . . . .
'The plot! the plot!' I hear you say.
Very well. I'll do my task
And briefly give you what you ask.
No one knew that Lady Dedlock
Bore a daughter out of wedlock;
No one knew the very one
Was saintly Esther Summerson.
Thanks to crossing-sweeper Jo,
By the novel's end we *know*.

'There must be more,' my reader cries.
Let him try to summarize
So long a work by such a writer.
That will teach the silly blighter.

PAUL GRIFFIN

CHARLES DICKENS:
A Christmas Carol

Ebenezer Scrooge
Was nobody's stooge;
It drove him into one of his rages
When somebody asked for more wages.

Bob Cratchit
Was especially liable to catch it
For expecting his pay
To cover Christmas Day.

But a series of Christmas spectres,
Acting as Scrooge's spiritual directors,
Asked him who was the cripple: Tiny Tim?
Or him?

And suddenly he became a hearty
Benefactor at the Cratchits' Christmas party.
Trade unions may boast,
But the best negotiator is a ghost.

PAUL GRIFFIN

CHARLES DICKENS:
David Copperfield

Steerforth, for all his dazzling looks, with rottenness is
    burning up,
While old Micawber gravely waits for something that is
    turning up.
How do they figure in one book? That's not a very easy
    one,
Because we have to add to them Uriah Heep (the greasy
    one),
Barkis who's willing, Mr Dick, and every single Peggotty,
Aunt Betsey Trotwood, of whose love our hero is the
    legatee,
And many more. Let's sum it up, and put our rhymes and
    puns away:
Our hero, David Copperfield, is born, and later runs away.
He prospers, and he marries twice; his ladies do not
    capture us,
But all his other friends and foes make every moment
    rapturous.
At nearly half a million words the novel's hardly cursory,
But it is fit (I trumpet it!) for nunnery or nursery.

PAUL GRIFFIN

CHARLES DICKENS:
Great Expectations

Dear Mr Dickens,

I enclose the first draft of a children's story which I think
may do well if illustrated properly. I hope you will agree that the story
is interesting and that I have managed to make the language not too
demanding. Perhaps it needs fleshing out a bit? I would be grateful
for your comments and look forward to hearing from you.

Yours *etc*.

Here is Pip. Here is Pip's big sister. Pip's big sister is married to Joe the blacksmith. See Pip's big sister frown.

Here comes a convict. Can Pip see the convict? Look out, Pip! The convict wants a pie. Fetch, Pip, fetch. Fetch the convict a pie. See Pip pinch the pie.

Pip sees a big old house. Pip goes into the big old house. Here is Pocket. Pocket tries to punch Pip. Pip punches Pocket. 'Be my pal, Pip,' says Pocket.

Here is Estella. Estella lives in the big old house. She is very pretty, thinks Pip. Pip meets a funny old lady in the big old house. Isn't she a funny old lady? She is not very pretty, thinks Pip. 'Hurt Pip, Estella!' says the funny old lady.

Pip grows up. Grow, Pip, grow. Pip gets some money. Where does Pip's money come from? Guess, Pip, guess. Pip cannot guess. Hasn't Pip become smart? See smart Pip. See ragged Joe. 'Go to London, Pip,' says Joe.

See who Pip meets in London. It is Pocket. Pip is surprised. Pip and Pocket have fun together. Estella comes to London too. Pip is pleased. Estella hurts Pip in London. Poor Pip.

Where is Pip going now? He is going back to see poor old Joe. Pip goes to see the funny old lady in the big old house too. Pip says goodbye to the funny old lady. Pip comes away. Can you see the big old house burning? Burn, house, burn. Quick, Pip! Pop back! Pip pops back. Poor Pip is too late. Poor old lady.

Pip goes back to London. Who is this sitting in Pip's chair? It is the convict! See Pip jump. He is surprised. See smart Pip. See the rough convict. 'Did you like the money, Pip?' says the convict.

Pip is surprised. See Pip's face. The convict is Estella's daddy. What a surprise for Pip.

Here come some men. They want to catch the convict. Quick, Pip, quick. Hide the convict. Help the convict get away, Pip. Oh, Pip! Too late again. The men take Pip's convict back to prison.

Pip's convict is not very well. Poor convict. Pip is very sad. All Pip's money has gone too. Poor Pip. 'What a lot I have learnt,' says Pip.

Here is Estella again. She says goodbye to Pip. Goodbye, Pip. Goodbye, Estella.

N.J.WARBURTON

CHARLES DICKENS:
Nicholas Nickleby

At Dotheboys Hall, Nick's a teacher,
It's ghastly, but matters soon reach a
    Head, and (three cheers!)
    Nick thrashes old Squeers,
And clears off with Smike, the poor creature.

They then join a Theatrical Co.;
Vincent Crummles, the seasoned old pro,
    Finds Nick splendid indeed
    As the juvenile lead,
And is sad when they both have to go.

Uncle Ralph, wicked brother of Daddy's,
Gets mad when the chivalrous lad is
    In time to save Kate
    From a terrible fate,
For all of Ralph's buddies are baddies.

Nick then falls for sweet Madeline Bray,
Who is destined, should Ralph have his way,
    To become the young bride
    Of the usurer, Gride –
But then comes the surprise *exposé*.

Nick watches Smike die, rather tearfully,
And Ralph, being found out so fearfully,
    Commits suicide,
    And the murder of Gride
Makes everything end very cheerfully.

JOYCE JOHNSON

CHARLES DICKENS:
Oliver Twist

Ollie's poor,
Asks for more
    Workhouse gruel.

Bumble the beadle
Gets the (dead) needle –
    Very cruel.

Twist runs off,
Short of scoff;
    In despair.

Joins a mob,
Taught to rob
    In Fagin's lair.

Out on a job
With Sikes (a yob)
    Twist is shot.

Finds kind friends,
Hardship ends
    (Tale does not).

Monks (a mystery)
Knows Twist's history.
    Harbours schemes.

Pretty Nancy
(Sikes's fancy)
    Spills the beans.

Vengeful Sikes
(Whom no one likes)
    Kills his girl.

Hue and cry!
Next to die
     Is Sikes, the churl.

Fagin's topped,
Monks is shopped,
     Makes confession:

Twist's his brother,
(Different mother);
     Long obsession

To ruin Ollie
And grab the lolly
     Left by Dad.

Twist's next option
Is adoption
     (Very glad).

Monks, the fraud,
Goes abroad:
     Dies in jail.

Bumble's fate?
The Workhouse Gate.
     End of tale.

RON RUBIN

CHARLES DICKENS:
Our Mutual Friend

Society thrills to a Will and a spill
When a news-splash is *CASH* and a *BODY*,
With Veneering appearing, though sneering, on hearing
The coffin gilds Boffin (A Noddy).
That river as quivers with rotters delivers
A quota for boaters that baffles,
And a peg-leg called Wegg gets licence to beg,

Which the wittering fritterer snaffles.
The Man with No Name sets his aim on a dame
Who is icy, but nicer when melted,
And a fool at a School starts to drool as a rule
On a pearl of a girl, till he's belted
By Fate, here in wait with its bait for the great
Or the small, for it's all True to Life,
Since the Poor get a raw deal, so low is the Law,
And each good guy's apprised of a wife.
Without dust you go bust in this book, it's unjust
But that passion for ash is essential.
Since the prose goes to show those with gold in their nose
How it's doom to the human potential.
An odd chap like Podsnap and associate sods clap
The itch of the rich for more readies
But the folk who go broke are the ones that they poke
In the crud and the mud as it eddies
Down the Thames that condemns all the helpless it hems
Between mean and unclean greedy banks.
This sickens C. Dickens, whose plot quickly thickens:
There's a rank smell of swells in its ranks.
Non-pilfering Wilfer who doesn't feel ill for
His daughter's the sort you applaud,
And Twemlow, a meek, rather weak old antique,
Is a sort who is thought above board.
But the money-mad, looby and rubicund boobies,
Like their lolly-crazed follies, are blamed;
And truly, there's few over whom you'd boo-hoo,
Including the two that I've named;
Indeed, as we say cheero! the hero, from zero
Gets oodles of boodle. Perpend:
Though you can't grease the palm of the charmer, John
    Harmon,
He's no suitable Mutual Friend.

BILL GREENWELL

CHARLES DICKENS:
The Pickwick Papers

Mr Jingle explains:

Pickwick – cheery old buffer – too dull in Dulwich –
founds Club – peregrinatory – peripatetical – tours England – three
cronies – capital fellows – finds factotum – sharp as a razor – sharper –
meets me – spellbound – down to Dingley Dell – spanking Christmas –
misunderstanding – I lose Mr P.'s good opinion – Mr P. takes digs
in town – amorous Landlady – breach of promise – put up to it by
pettifoggers – case tried – Sam sauces judge – diverting – exceedingly –
Buzfuz cross-examines – better actor than Kean – gets no change out
of Sam – but jury – muttonheads! – find for plaintiff – outrageous –
dames fearful – Mr P. refuses to cough up – incarcerated in Fleet –
finds me there – generous – magnanimous too – very – (*sob, sob*) forgive
me! – don't often weep – but Mr P. – a prince of men – adventures
too many to tell – extremely various – always hilarious – some
nefarious – breaks into girls' school at night – caught – tricky! – very –
in bed with yellow curl-papers – Ipswich – fishy – (Mr P. a sly dog?) –
all ends well – bless you, Pickwick!

MARTIN FAGG

SIR ARTHUR CONAN DOYLE:
The Hound of the Baskervilles

The Hell-Hound

Beware, beware the fiendish hound that haunts the moors of Devon,
That's cursed the House of Baskerville since sixteen forty-seven!
Inquire not too closely what it is nor whence it came,
Nor whose those blazing evil eyes and jaws of dripping flame.

For it was on the very night that bad Sir Hugo sold
His soul unto the Evil One – his body, stiff and cold,
Was found upon the moor, and close beside it, black as night,
There stood this savage monster. Those who saw it died of fright.

And in this present century, strange stories still are heard.
The sudden death of good Sir Charles – who knows how that occurred?
Stark fear was writ upon his face, they found him on the ground,
And by his lifeless body was the footprint of a hound.

And those who live upon the moor, both sane and superstitious,
Have heard a demoniac moan, half mournful and half vicious,
The weirdest sound that ever yet assailed the mortal ear,
That filled them with foreboding and a thrill of nameless fear.

But now this spectral demon-dog the moor no longer roams;
It has been slain by no one less than Mr Sherlock Holmes.
Then what its parentage, you ask, and what its damned abode?
The mongrel came from Ross & Mangles, dealers, Fulham Road,
And as for that unearthly flame that caused stout hearts to faint,
A mortal hand had daubed its coat with phosphorescent paint.

JOYCE JOHNSON

ALEXANDRE DUMAS (Dumas *père*):
The Three Musketeers

'. . . you can say what you like too many people let their
minds sort of go to seed after a certain age the wife and I went to
evening classes again last winter we took French literature and *The
Three Musketeers* was the set piece by this fantastic writer Victor
Hugo it seems he had this terrific output of plays and stories and
books there was this boastful *Garçon* called D'Artagnan came to Paris
and picked fights with these three musketeers Athos Porthos and
Araminta anyway he became a musketeer himself and they all used
to swagger through the streets of Paris shouting and singing and
stabbing people it seems he was in a position to service the Queen and
there was this vicious bitch Milady de Winter who killed the Duke of
Buckingham and she got her come-uppance alright don't you worry
and D'Artagnan was rewarded by the King what sort of puzzles me
is why the book is called *The Three Musketeers* when there were four
of them it was a mistake in translation from the original if you ask me

and why were they called musketeers when all they used were these fantastic swords the whole course had a really terrific broadening effect on our minds and now we've got European literature out of the way next winter we're taking Chinese ceramics . . .'

T.L.McCARTHY

DAPHNE DU MAURIER:
Rebecca

Lucky Mrs Max de Winter
Had a husband with a minter
Money, who would never stinter
    (Very poor she'd been),
But as soon as she got inter
Manderley, she felt a hinter
First wife's power to imprinter
    Image on the scene;

Relatives and friends assesser
As unquestionably lesser
Than her brilliant predecesser,
   In whose fancy gear
Mrs Danvers (chief aggresser)
Carefully contrives to dresser –
Aims to shock him and distresser
   But the crunch is near . . .

Far from worshipping Rebecca
Max has stuffed beneath the decca
Murdered body, till a wrecca
   Boat and corpse reclaims.
Fearful at the doc's they checca,
Find a cause for deathward trecca
Lucky break, so back for brecca –

   Manderley's in flames!

MARY HOLTBY

LAWRENCE DURRELL:
The Alexandria Quartet

In the *Quartet* Durrell tells
Of Alexandria's sights and smells,
Giving strange rococo names
To his multinational dames
And his men, who never quite
Know with whom to spend the night:
Sick Melissa, Greek and lean,
Jewish, insolent Justine,
Clea, English, milky-white,
Liza, lacking only sight,
Pursewarden, using words like paint,
Scobie, who becomes a saint,
Mountolive, who is Leila's dream,
Balthazar, Narouz, Nessim:
All these wander in and out
Crying: 'What is life about?'
Darley/Durrell doesn't know,
Tells us we had better go
Where the truth is plain to see,
To the works of Cavafy.
Of those works I cannot speak;
They are in demotic Greek.

PAUL GRIFFIN

GEORGE ELIOT:
Middlemarch

Mr Brooke summarises:

My niece Dorothea, clever for a woman – changeable –
interested in reform, cottages, that sort of thing – I went in for that a
good deal myself at one time – but I pulled up, I saw it would not do.
But Dorothea – she married, you know – Casaubon – learned fellow –
ought to have been a bishop – was writing a scholarly work – like
Aquinas – you know Aquinas? – I knew – no, Casaubon and my niece –
had fits, you know – studies affected him – called in a doctor –

Lydgate – knew his uncle – clever fellow – tried to make scientific discoveries – blood, experiments, that sort of thing – I went in for science once, but I saw it would not do; science takes you too far over the hedge – Lydgate pulled up; wrote about gout – married, you know – Mayor's daughter – fine girl – sister of Fred Vincy, writes about agriculture – turnips, potatoes, like Cobbett, Virgil, that sort of thing – *quid faciat laetas segetes* – the Georgics, that's a fine thing – married too – like my niece and Ladislaw – I spoke strongly, I told her it was a hampering thing, marriage – never married myself. Clever fellow, Ladislaw, like Shelley – reform, equality; went in for that a good deal myself at one time. Connected with Bulstrode, you know – curious story, one's gain another's loss, like in political economy. Though some say that it all balances out; I've argued that myself. Sent Ladislaw all my documents – could make a book – like Eliot. You know Eliot? – wrote novels – went too far, though – should have reined in . . .

REM BEL

GEORGE ELIOT:
The Mill on the Floss

There's trouble at t' mill caused by Wakem,
Who, Tulliver claims, wants to break 'em;
    While Maggie's great joy
    Is to court Wakem's boy,
'Such liaisons,' says Tom, 'you shan't make 'em.'

Stephen Guest makes her error much greater –
He's charming and eager to date 'er;
    And poor crippled Phil
    Feels the desolate chill
Of rejection in love, but can't hate 'er.
A boat ride with Stephen proves fateful,
For Maggie feels wretched, not grateful;
    She stoutly says: 'No'
    To stirrings below,
Then she drowns in a flood, which is hateful.

TIM HOPKINS

T. S. ELIOT:
Murder in the Cathedral

To the Chairwoman,
Canterbury Townswomen's Guild

Dear Madam,

My attention has been drawn to the action of your
members in indulging in illegal poetry recitations around the
cathedral in order to welcome back to our shores a certain clergyman,
sometimes known as the Archbishop of Canterbury. This is one of
the two things it is forbidden to do in the streets and frightens the
horses. The speaking of unrhymed free verse, with the constant
repetition of such phrases as 'Woe, woe' is highly confusing to the
aforementioned quadrupeds.

I am,

Your obedient servant,

Ivor Truncheon,

Chief Constable

To the Chairwoman,
Canterbury Townswomen's Guild

Dear Madam,

I had occasion to reprimand you recently regarding the
contravention by your members of certain by-laws prohibiting the
recital of poetry in public places likely to lead to disturbance of the
peace.

I regret to have to inform you that further similar incidents
have now occurred. When approached by my officers, your members
said that they had witnessed certain temptations of the aforesaid
Archbishop by certain supernatural apparitions.

I would point out that the presence of your members on the Cathedral steps is a temptation of another and far more serious sort.

Yours faithfully,

Ivor Truncheon,

Chief Constable

To the Chairwoman,
Canterbury Townswomen's Guild

Dear Madam,

I have to refer to your protest regarding the accidental death of a local clergyman while assisting some officials of the King's peace with their legitimate inquiries. I would point out that such unfortunate incidents may occur when persons resist being taken into custody for their own good.

I would like to point out that displays of public grief are forbidden. On the other hand brief cries, such as 'Long Live Henry the Second' or 'The police are doing a fine job', are quite legal. In any case, it would be better for your members to get on with their avowed occupation as charwomen and clean up any remaining blood stains.

The matter was one of National Security, and in these cases it is the Government who must inform the courts whether any crime has been committed.

I am,

Yours etc.

Sir I. Truncheon, Bt.,

Chief Constable

E.O.PARROTT

T. S. ELIOT:
The Waste Land

I

In April one seldom feels cheerful;
Dry stones, sun and dust make me fearful;
    Clairvoyantes distress me,
    Commuters depress me –
Met Stetson and gave him an earful.

II

She sat on a mighty fine chair,
Sparks flew as she tidied her hair;
    She asks many questions,
    I make few suggestions –
Bad as Albert and Lil – what a pair!

III

The Thames runs, bones rattle, rats creep;
Tiresias fancies a peep –
    A typist is laid,
    A record is played –
Wei la la. After this it gets deep.

IV

A Phoenician called Phlebas forgot
About birds and his business – the lot,
    Which is no surprise
    Since he'd met his demise
And been left in the ocean to rot.

V

No water. Dry rocks and dry throats,
Then thunder, a shower of quotes
    From the Sanskrit and Dante.
    Da. Damyata. Shantih.
I hope you'll make sense of the notes.

WENDY COPE

T. S. ELIOT:
The Waste Land

Spring's a lousy time, reviving
Heart-throbs one thought had been forgotten.
But life is like that, bloody
Awful when you stop to think about it.
Crawling, fog-bound, over London Bridge,
Going for a picnic up the Thames,
Stopping for a quick one in a pub,
Seducing a typist in a flat,
Tout c'est la même chose. La vie, c'est terrible.
Da.
Damn.

STANLEY J. SHARPLESS

DEAN FARRAR:
Eric, or Little by Little

In a Manx school,
Quite a swanks' school,
Dwelt a minor, made for Sin;
Eric – boarder –
Just adored a
Furtive fag and double-gin!

Soon he skipped prayers,
Used the back stairs,
Sneaking out to haunt the town;
Thought old Euclid
Was quite putrid –
Fluffed his exams – was kept down!

Then he missed 'nets'
Placing his bets;
Met rough types who tend to welch!
Drank from slippers
Of Manx strippers;
Came in late – was heard to belch!

When he's fervent
With a servant –
How much lower can he sink?
For the trespass,
'DRUNK IN VESPERS',
Is sent home – just dodging clink!

When he gets there
In a bath-chair,
Cries his ma: 'You're bonkers too;
Girls and brandy
Were too handy,
School and pool ain't good for you!'

PASCO POLGLAZE

HENRY FIELDING:
Tom Jones

Tom Jones, Tom Jones, you're short of a dad,
    All along, down along, out along lea;
Though you may be a wild 'un, you're never a bad,
Like Mr Blifil, Mr Thwackum, Mr Square, Black George, old
        roaring Squire Western and all.

Grow up, little Thomas, not yet good as gold,
    All along, down along, out along lea;
There are men to be wrestled, and girls to be rolled,
Like Mrs Waters, Mrs Fitzpatrick, Lady Bellaston and
        anyone female at all.

Sophia the faithful is waiting afar,
    All along, down along, out along lea;
Till you grow out of wandering, and find who you are,
From Mr Partridge, Mrs Waters, Mrs Miller, your uncle
        Squire Allworthy and all.

PAUL GRIFFIN

EDWARD FITZGERALD (Trans.):
The Rubáiyát of Omar Khayyám

> Wake up, to drink
> But not to think;
> Life simply isn't viable.
> The world is odd
> And so is God,
> But Persian plonk's reliable.

>> PAUL GRIFFIN

> The Rubáiyát
> Of Omar Khayyám has a shy at
> The riddle of what life is all about.
> The answer's nowt.

>> PETER VEALE

F. SCOTT FITZGERALD:
The Great Gatsby

> Nick Carraway and Gatsby (Jay)
> Are next-door neighbours; every day
> The enigmatic Gatsby gazes
> Towards a distant green light (Daisy's).

> He throws wild parties; round his pond
> Collects the New York *demi-monde*.
> They rarely meet their host, who mopes
> Indoors, but innocently hopes

> That somewhere in this crowd of liggers,
> Drunks, bores and Charlestoning gold-diggers,
> He'll spot a girl who drove him crazy
> Before the Great War – name of Daisy.

> Mrs Buchanan now, her life
> Is wasted as the unloved wife
> Of brutish Tom (who has a manic
> Mistress, wife of a mechanic).

They meet; it changes both their lives.
Intoxicated, Daisy drives
The Rolls from town; sadly they hurtle
Into Tom's manic mistress, Myrtle.

To shield the guilty loved one's name,
Impulsive Gatsby takes the blame.
(And that's how idealistic fools
End up face down in swimming pools.)

PETER NORMAN

E. M. FORSTER:
A Passage to India

Dr Aziz and Miss Quested,
While the picnic party rested,
Wandered through the bat-infested
Caves of Malabar and jested.
Was she *actually* divested
Of her virtue, as she thought?

Dr Aziz and Miss Quested –
She, though frightfully flat-chested,
Odd vibrations manifested.
Could it *really* be suggested
That the Doctor had molested
Such a virgin overwrought?

Dr Aziz and Miss Quested –
When the Doctor was arrested,
Mrs Moore, of course, protested . . .
But the reader, sorely tested,
Is a lot more interested
In *this* aspect of the plot:

Dr Aziz and Miss Quested –
Did he give her one or not?

T.L.McCARTHY

MRS GASKELL:
Cranford

Cranford is written by an 'I'
Who casts a keen but kindly eye
Upon the strict propriety
Of an enclosed society,
Its regulated *bonhomie*
And elegant economy.

Here's poverty with genteel face;
Here's lavender – but as for lace,
When this is swallowed by the cat,
We give her an emetic – that
Restores the lace to human view
Which, washed and dried, looks good as new.

Here's Mrs Jamieson, the Hon.,
And Lady Glenmire. Later on
She much offends her snobby sister
By marrying a simple Mr.
We have a most exciting scare
Of robberies, which never were.

The business world does not intrude.
We scorn the vulgar and the rude;
But when that dreadful bank goes bust,
We realize Miss Matty must
Sell teas (those of the highest grade),
And none of us dares call it 'trade'.

An Aga comes into the shop;
Miss Matty gazes, fit to drop.
It can't be – yes, it *is* none other
Than Peter, her own long-lost brother!
We leave them both in happy ease,
There's no more need to purvey teas.

JOYCE JOHNSON

EDWARD GIBBON:
The History of the Decline and Fall of the Roman Empire

The fall and decline
of the Roman Empire
into the mire,
started with Trajan
and the awful Antonines,
basically . . . swines.

Of Justinian,
few of us tend to have a
sound opinion,
and boring Charlemagne,
sent the Holy Roman camp
further down the drain.

To allow themselves
to be outwitted by Turks,
the Romans were berks;
Moslems arrived,
fierce and unscrupulous,
so . . . few survived.

Empires endure
when one learns to play cricket,
and keep one's heart pure.
Put another way,
if they had been gentlemen,
they'd be here today.

RUSSELL LUCAS

NIKOLAI GOGOL:
The Government Inspector

In Tsarist days, without so much as 'by your leave' or 'please',
    At any time inspectors might appear;
And few words terrified the local rulers more than these:
    'The Tsar's Inspector-General is here!'

The Governor of one small town mistook a travelling man,
    One Khlestakov, a minor bureaucrat,
For such a high official, and the man conceived a plan
    Enabling him to benefit from that.

He meddled here, inspected there, devoid of all restraint,
    Eating and drinking everything in sight,
Collected from the merchants their petitions of complaint,
    Accepting heavy bribes to put things right.

The daughter of the Governor accepted his proposal,
    (Although he'd only offered it in jest!)
He asked to have a team of horses put at his disposal
    ('The ones that gallop fastest would be best!')

By fiddling with the outward mail, the true facts came to light,
    For Khlestakov confided in a friend.
The citizens, with words obscene and gestures impolite,
    Claimed that the Governor was round the bend.

The Governor's grand house was filled with noisy malcontents,
    With functionaries blaming one another.
The merchants spoke of bribery and lawless incidents.
    The daughter wailed, assisted by her mother.

Outside the house, among the crowd, a further tumult spread.
    A gendarme made the situation clear:
The man stood to attention and saluted: 'Sir,' he said,
    'The *real* Inspector-General is here!'

T.L.McCARTHY

WILLIAM GOLDING:
Lord of the Flies

On an island made of coral,
    Life was organised and fine.
        Ralph and Peterkin and Jack

Never seemed to have a quarrel;
    So said R. M. Ballantyne.
        Golding turns that on its back.

Jack, Ralph, Piggy, all of Golding's
    Boys marooned without a master,
        Demonstrate their evil will,
When they're free of adult scoldings,
    Gallop downhill ever faster,
        Fight and bully, even kill.

Any worship must be beastly
    In the general malarkus;
        Choirboy Simon, half insane,
Finds himself a sort of priestly
    Role before a porcine carcass;
        Beelzebub is king again.

Golding means in all this antic,
    We should recognize our features;
        Humanity breeds war and noise.
News, perhaps, if you're romantic;
    Not to parents or to teachers
        Or anyone who's used to boys.

PAUL GRIFFIN

KENNETH GRAHAME:
The Wind in the Willows

The wind in the willows ...
Spring-cleaning for Mole;
The Rat's on the river,
The Toad's in a hole –

Demoniac driver,
How rashly he boasted
Who, battered and roasted
For past peccadilloes,
Lies flumped on the floor . . .

The ways of the Wood . . .
The darkness, the scuffle
Of sinister paws,
The snowdrifts that muffle,
The bramble that claws;
The whistling, the faces
In heart-stopping places;
The signs understood –
The scraper, the door . . .

The heist of the Hall . . .
The Toad's out of prison
(By cheek, train, and barge),
But weasels have risen
And stoats are at large.
The kin of Archdeacons
Despairs not, nor weakens,
When Badger's in charge –
Ratastrophic, uproarious,
See virtue victorious
And enemies fall!
How tranquil once more
The wind in the willows . . .

MARY HOLTBY

KENNETH GRAHAME:
The Wind in the Willows

The Diary of A. Mole

March 21st. Half-way through spring-cleaning when I realized what a middle-class thing it was to be doing. The Mole family has always been bound by convention: it makes me sick. Decided to go up for some air and met Ratty. Joined him in a feast. He has no inhibitions about gluttony. I had a little, which was a relief because I was beginning to think I was anorexic.

March 25th. I wouldn't want to be as nosy as Ratty, but I wish I had his confidence. He took me to see his friend Toad. Very upper-class, jolly and self-indulgent. Came away feeling tainted by bourgeois values.

April 3rd. Caravanning with Ratty and Toad. He is like Marie-Antoinette with his fads and whims. There is no doubt that he's quite potty. Anyway, it didn't last because he saw a car and now that's all he can think about. It's rather distasteful to see what money can do to an animal. I suggested the discarded caravan could go to Oxfam, but he wasn't even listening. Noticed more spots this morning.

April 8th. Ratty and I went to see Badger. Badger is really wise and I have decided to model myself on him, retaining my individuality, of course. He is very cultured but lives in a genuine working-class area. I nearly asked him what he does about spots but thought better of it. He thinks we should lock Toad in his room.

April 15th. Toad has escaped, which merely confirms my original diagnosis. Wealth has made him mad. Still, with Toad Hall now empty and stoats and ferrets living in cramped conditions, there is an ideal opportunity for a bit of social movement. I said this to Ratty but I don't think he heard.

May 2nd. An amazing discovery. Ratty is a drug addict! We were out for a row and he started hallucinating about some weird creature playing some pipes. After some consideration I have decided to overlook this flaw in Ratty. Maybe I can help him. Still no sign of Toad – or the spots going.

May 15th. Ratty has found Toad! Very much a mixed blessing, I think. He has been in prison for stealing cars, has dabbled in transvestism and is officially on the run. I suppose his wealth will keep him from the fate he deserves. It's disgusting, really. I only wish he didn't make me laugh so much.

May 17th. Just as I predicted, the Wild Wooders have taken over Toad Hall. Unfortunately, they are not the decent working-class types I thought they might be. Badger says we should enter the place by a secret tunnel and take them by surprise. I wonder whether I am a coward or not. Some more spots have appeared. Is this because I am worried about getting into a fight, or because I am worried about the spots?

May 30th. What cannot be achieved by a small but determined band from different social backgrounds with a single objective in mind? I must admit I feel quite proud of myself. I'm still not sure whether it was an act of true socialism to reinstate Toad, though. And I haven't noticed the spots fading yet.

N.J.WARBURTON

GRAHAM GREENE:
Brighton Rock

Stroppy little Pinkie,
Catholic and kinky,
Was cock of his petty little walk.
He heard a little bird
Had seen what had occurred,
So he thought they ought to have a little talk.

The silly little judy
Was feeling very broody;
She took one look at him and fell in love.
So when a big fat Ida
Sat down beside her,
She gave the meddling so-and-so the shove.

But Ida was his nemesis;
She moved round licensed premises,
And laughed: 'That little sod's a lot to learn!'
Embattled, Pinkie said:
'I'm better wed than dead,
And – one up on St Paul – I'll marry *and* burn!'

Theologically crammed,
He thought they both were damned,
And tried to organize a suicide pact.
But, though he lost his life,
He left his little wife
With a disc that was a little short on tact.

PETER NORMAN

GRAHAM GREENE:
Brighton Rock

Hale didn't feel so hearty when he met the razor gang
And got his ticket punched for good and all.
He went out with a whimper, not a devastating bang,
But his end, it was the start of Pinkie's fall.

Now a juvenile delinquent wearing acne on his face,
And the merest bit of bum-fluff on his chin,
Might seem banal, but Pinkie had a special kind of grace,
On account of being intimate with sin.

Whereas Ida, Pinkie's nemesis, all lipstick, rouge and port,
Was your classic interfering humanist.
She was all for right and wrong as they're conventionally
   taught,
But the deeper metaphysics she just missed.

She was out to rescue Rose – that's Pinkie's innocent young
   wife –
From a life of squalor, misery and crime;
But her intervention cost the poor satanic boy his life,
Meaning Rose was widowed long before her time.

She went off with the disc she'd got her husband to record
(Little knowing she would hear his dying curse) –
While Ida settled down to meddle with her ouija board
In her average, sensual, Godless universe.

BASIL RANSOME-DAVIES

GRAHAM GREENE:
The Quiet American

Once upon a time, in the faraway country of Vietnam,
there lived a man called Mr Fowler.

His job was writing stories for the newspaper about
different lots of people who were getting very cross with each other.

Mr Fowler's best friend was a nice lady called Phuong.
He was very kind to her and let her share his bed.

Then, a quiet man called Mr Pyle arrived from America
and Mr Pyle and Mr Fowler became sort of chums. Mr Pyle liked
Phuong as well and said he would like her to sleep in his bed which
made Mr Fowler frown.

One day, Mr Pyle got some plastic things which he said
were to make toys for poor Vietnamese children.

Mr Fowler found out that the toys sometimes went
BANG and made people very poorly.

A bit later, Mr Pyle was very brave and rescued Mr Fowler
from some nasty men which made Mr Fowler feel a bit awkward.

Then nice Phuong went to live with brave Mr Pyle.

Another day there was a big bang in the High Street and
lots of people fell down and never got up again. Mr Fowler thought
it might be because of Mr Pyle's toys, so he told another man, who
didn't like Mr Pyle, where Mr Pyle was going for a walk.

The next day Mr Pyle was found in a river and he was very
quiet indeed.

So nice Phuong went back to Mr Fowler who had got a letter from Mrs Fowler saying she did not mind Phuong being Mr Fowler's special friend.

Without poor Mr Pyle around, Mr Fowler and Phuong could live happily ever after.

Do you think they did?

V. ERNEST COX

GEORGE AND WEEDON GROSSMITH: The Diary of a Nobody

I am sorry I ever let Carrie talk me into trying to get this Diary published. Seventeen rejections have dampened my spirits. Sometimes it is returned with the curtest of notes, sometimes not at all, so that I have to go to the publisher's office to retrieve it. On the last such occasion, an insolent young pup of a clerk rushed into an inner office, bellowing 'He's here, Mr Ponsford!', whereupon a fat, dandified individual emerged and stood gazing at me as if I were something in a cage in Regent's Park.

But now, hope. This evening, Lupin brought home to supper (no one dresses a salad like my Carrie!) a colleague who has just joined his firm. He introduced him as 'Pongo' Nettleton – though this can hardly be the name he was given at the font. This 'Pongo' is, according to Lupin, not only a sporting light baritone, an intrepid bicyclist and an inspired speculator but up to a hundred other 'dodges' and 'wheezes' (his terminology, not mine). Apparently, he now thinks of starting his own small publishing house and is on the look-out for promising material. He said, in rather superior tones, that though he was far too busy to read actual manuscripts, he would be pleased to consider my Diary if I could give him the gist of it on half a sheet of notepaper.

I thought this odd in a budding publisher but, leaving them in the parlour, did as 'Pongo' requested. I wrote that this was simply the Diary of fifteen months in the life of a typical proud but humble Englishman who worked daily in the City and returned each evening to his darling wife and his home, sweet home, on the airy heights of Holloway. It told of their enterprising if wayward son, Lupin, their old friends Cummings and Gowing, and of the hundred amusing or annoying incidents that mark everyday existence. Boring to some, no doubt, but – here I was interrupted by a most extraordinary commotion. Rushing back into the parlour, I found 'Pongo' rolling in convulsions on the hearth-rug. I thought it must be food-poisoning (though the supper crab had seemed quite fresh and wholesome), but Lupin explained that 'Pongo' had decided to read the Diary after all and was merely helpless with laughter. A gratifying reaction, no doubt, in one way, but I cannot help feeling a shade uneasy about it in another . . .

MARTIN FAGG

GEORGE AND WEEDON GROSSMITH: The Diary of a Nobody

Sunday
Sent Sarah out this morning to Smith's to purchase all the Sunday papers, which we do not usually take, and then found it necessary to excise and burn large parts of them. After lunch (a tender piece of cold mutton) I settled down to read the 'reviews' (as they are called in literary circles – I must begin to learn these terms). I was utterly astounded to find my Diary described in one quite reputable journal as a 'comic masterpiece' and in others relegated to the columns dealing with works of a facetious or humorous nature. It must be that one of Mr Agnew's young men had sent copies to the wrong persons for review. I explained as much to Carrie after I had shown her a few of the articles, but she only smiled oddly and went off to see her aunt, the one in Camberwell.

It is really most strange. My Diary is a sober and factual account of some incidents in the private life of a rising man of business and although not devoid of humour – indeed, some of my jokes are quite good – can surely not be called 'comic'! In particular, one person writes about the time when I painted the bath red, saying that it caused him to 'roll on the floor', and I can see little to laugh at in the incident, although it certainly inculcated a moral lesson about the unwisdom of undertaking work properly belonging to a working man.

I very much fear that there may be unfortunate repercussions. Neither Mr Perkupp, who is the head of my office, nor our son Lupin's new parents-in-law, who are most respectable people, will relish appearance in a 'comic' work and they will complain. And I fear my good friends, Cummings and Gowing, will

feel able to take revenge for my comments on their own rather
lamentable sense of humour.

JOHN STANLEY SWEETMAN

DASHIELL HAMMETT:
The Glass Key

Life seems full of sacrifices when election time is near.
You may find that little crises threaten what you hold most dear. Even
friends whose love you treasure temporise with 'ifs' and 'buts', while
your enemies take pleasure sticking guns into your guts. Homicide
becomes the fashion, like the latest hat or gown, for in the heat of
human passion morals may be melted down. All of us must bear such
crosses: do not cry or blame ill-luck. Like Ned Beaumont, cut your
losses, grab the girl and run like fuck.

BASIL RANSOME-DAVIES

DASHIELL HAMMETT:
The Maltese Falcon

Take a pair of San Francisco private eyes.
Subtract the one who dies in chapter two.
Add one rare bird, the much-contended prize,
And one demure, deceptive *ingénue*.

The problems grow and multiply by reams.
Two cops give Samuel Spade the third degree.
The heavies are divided as each schemes
To cheat and double-cross the other three.

The plot is algebra, the French would say;
So many unknown factors must be guessed.
What really counts is knowing how to play
The angles: only Sam can pass this test.

Equations balance when our rugged hero
Has cancelled out the sum of villainy,
And proved the famous falcon just a zero,
And got his girlfriend's number. QED.

BASIL RANSOME-DAVIES

THOMAS HARDY:
Jude the Obscure

Marygreen

Dear Claire,

I really fancy this dishy man in our village, but he don't
seem to notice me. All he's interested in is book-learning. I am
attractive and have quite a good job cutting up pigs. How can I let
him know my true feelings?

Dear Arabella: Be bold, for both your sakes. Your young man is too
wrapped up in education and needs you to bring him out. Have you
thought of lobbing a bit of pig at him? If you managed to hit him with
a pig's more intimate areas I'm sure he'd notice you. It may sound
crude but I have known several men who have responded to this sort
of hint.

Marygreen

Dear Claire,

Please can you advise me? My wife tricked me into
marriage by pretending to be pregnant but now she says she wants to
leave me. I realize this would enable me to devote more time to my
studies but I can't help feeling guilty about letting her go.

Dear Jude: Don't be ashamed of your impulses. Education is a
wonderful thing and nothing to be embarrassed about. Let your wife
go and then take yourself off to the nearest university town. It sounds

fantastic, I know, but some colleges do take working men and if you are on the spot you never know what might turn up.

Shaston

Dear Claire,

I am a schoolmaster of some years' experience. The other day a former pupil of mine turned up out of the blue with a beautiful girl he claimed to be his cousin. I could see that he was fond of her, but I, too, find her to be most alluring. I try to forget her but can't. What can I do?

Dear Mr Phillotson: You are wrong to try and put this girl out of your mind. Age should be no barrier to genuine yearning. Don't feel bad about your rival. All's fair in love and war, you know, and a lot of women actually prefer older men.

Christminster

Dear Claire,

I have had the misfortune to fall in love with the beautiful wife of an older man. Apparently, she jumped out of his window the other evening in order to avoid his attentions, so I suspect she is not as happy with him as she pretends to be. Is it wrong of me to continue seeing her?

Dear Jude: Of course it's not wrong. Our impulses are often our best guide. I'm sure your young friend knows her own mind, and if she responds to your plight don't, whatever you do, feel guilty about it. You may save her from a disastrous relationship. After all, it's better for two people to find joy together than for three to continue in unhappiness.

Christminster

Dear Claire,

My mummy and daddy separated before I was born and now my mummy has handed me over to my daddy and his girlfriend. They are very kind to me but find it difficult to get a place to live because of me and the other children. This makes me miserable. What can I do to help?

Dear 'Father Time': I can't believe you are as young as you say: you sound very knowing to me so I'm going to be straight with you. Mummies and daddies sometimes need time together. The pressures of too many children can be quite harmful to their relationships. Isn't it about time you found some way to leave them alone for a while?

Christminster

Dear Claire,

I am feeling bad about having left my husband to move in with the man I love. Matters have come to a head since the son by his first wife hanged himself along with our own children. Does this indicate that I am wrong to be living with this man?

Dear Sue: You have got yourself in a pickle, haven't you? Marriage is a very precious thing, you know, but it isn't always the bed of roses people take it to be. You have to work at it. Surely the death of your children tells you this? I think you should return to your true husband and try to work something out. I enclose some leaflets that might be helpful.

Christminster

Dear Claire,

My man's girlfriend has gone back to her husband and he has come back to me. The trouble is I think he's still pining for her. I wouldn't mind but it's a nuisance, what with him hanging about in bed all day and me, naturally enough, wanting to be with more lively people. How can I put some 'go' into him without having to be with him all the time?

Dear Arabella: You are right to be out doing things. Perhaps your example will help your husband to snap out of it. He's bound to brood over the past if he doesn't occupy himself. You might suggest some correspondence courses. Education can be a wonderful tonic, you know.

N.J.WARBURTON

THOMAS HARDY:
The Mayor of Casterbridge

Never sell your wives to sailors when the booze is in the blood:
You may rise to civic honours, but your name will still be mud;
Rivals take your trade and profit, promised spouses let you down,
'Daughters' find their rightful fathers, ruin drives you from the town.
Lonely death at last shall take you whom all other friends refuse.
Better bear domestic boredom, better barricade the booze.

MARY HOLTBY

THOMAS HARDY:
Tess of the D'Urbervilles

One June, as strawberries were turning red,
Tess Durbeyfield, a middling fair young virgin,
Did find herself in cousin Alec's bed
('Twas not made clear how much she needed urging).

'Oh, Alec!' cried our Tess, 'how thou hast mastered me!
Let's make a babe and share connubial bliss!'
But D'Urberville was little short of dastardly;
Quoth he: ''Twas nothing but a playful kiss!'

She got with child – such things do come unplanned.
With that, her aspirations started narrowing.
She found work, breaking up the flinty land
(In every sense she found the experience harrowing).

Then things looked up – her next job wasn't bad:
Improving her complexion in a dairy.
And there she met an eligible lad –
Well-meaning, though a trifle airy-fairy.

Angel's delight was short-lived; when he learned
That Tess had had a taste of carnal pleasures,
He froze as ardently as he had burned,
Forcing her to resort to desperate measures!

Things ended badly (it's called Nemesis);
And – no less grim a fate for being tardy –
Straight to the gallows went the hapless Tess.
Well – what do you expect from Thomas Hardy?

PETER NORMAN

L. P. HARTLEY:
The Go-Between

In a fine Norfolk summer when passions ran high,
A sinewy lad cast a practical eye
On an upper-class blonde in a tight-fitting blouse,
Who sent him hot notes through a boy in her house.

It didn't occur to these victims of passion
That physical rapture, though sweet in its fashion,
Looks rather ungainly to immature witnesses,
And may even threaten their sexual fitnesses.

PAUL GRIFFIN

NATHANIEL HAWTHORNE:
The Scarlet Letter

During Boston's colonial days
Its rulers had punishing ways.
    In those Puritan times
    Acts of passion were crimes –
And the woman, you know, always pays.

Thus a lonely young wife, Hester Prynne,
Who'd committed adulterous sin,
    Was condemned to display
    A symbolical 'A';
But she wore it with pride, not chagrin.

Was the sentence severe, or condign?
Never mind! Hester flaunted this sign,
    But she guarded the name
    Of the man in the game:
Arthur Dimmesdale, a local divine.

It was he who had fathered the girl
That Hester so aptly named Pearl,
    But the torturing force
    Of an inward remorse
Soon had his poor mind in a whirl.

Then enter the vengeful physician –
Hester's husband – intent on a mission
    To wring the priest's heart
    With a devilish art,
And exploit his tormented condition.

Under pressure, the pastor is driven
To public confession. Then, shriven,
    He dies, free at last
    From the guilt of the past,
But can Chillingworth's crime be forgiven?

BASIL RANSOME-DAVIES

JOSEPH HELLER:
Catch 22

Catch Twenty-Two is a
Hell of a fine book, its
Principal character
Is an odd chap:
Captain Yossarian,
Nomenclaturally,
Doesn't like killing and
Thinks life is crap.

Whether in hospital,
Fooling psychiatrists,
Or fixing generals,
Yossar has style;
Knowing that warfare brings,
Super-abundantly,
Chances for heroes – and
Making a pile!

Kidding poor chaplains still
Pink from their colleges;
Baiting a colonel for
Being a creep;
Catching a nurse as she,
Hyper-imprudently,
Stoops by his bedside when
He's not asleep!

Milo flies bombers out
Just to get groceries,
Bottles of vino and
Gum for the crew!
Yep – the whole set-up is
Phantasmagorical –
Are they all dead? Is it
Catch Twenty-Two?

PASCO POLGLAZE

ERNEST HEMINGWAY:
For Whom the Bell Tolls

Oh, where have you been, Robert Jordan, my son,
So *ängstlich*, so *déraciné*?
Did you seek peace of mind at the point of a gun,
Happy to throw your life away?

Were your nights with Maria just as you said,
Moving the earth like J C B's?
Did you think twice, hearing El Sordo was dead?
Did slogans make you ill at ease?

And when Pablo betrayed the guerrilla band,
Did you become muted and fey?
Did you welcome the fate Pilar saw in your hand?
Was it a death-wish made you stay?

Did you want to go out in American style?
O, tell the truth, my son, my son;
Living all the way up for a short, short while
Till your life and your cause and your message were Donne.

BASIL RANSOME-DAVIES

ERNEST HEMINGWAY:
The Old Man and the Sea

There was an old man of the sea,
Who for eighty-four days went fish-free,
    But he rowed out next day,
    And almost straightway
Struck gold – piscatorially.

He could tell from the tug on the string
That this fish was no underling,
    So he held tight his rod,
    While the fish – awkward sod –
Took two days to have its last fling.

The old man was knackered, but still,
Killing it gave him a thrill.
Oh, what a darlin'!
An eighteen-foot marlin!
Much too big to go under the grill.

He'd just lashed the fish to his skiff,
When some sharks of its blood caught a whiff,
They homed in at speed,
Grabbed a take-away feed,
Leaving just the bare bones of the stiff.

He returned with the stripped skeleton,
Dragged his boat up the beach, whereupon
He heard a remark:
'Oh, look, a dead shark!'
An ironical note to end on.

V. ERNEST COX

HOMER:
The Iliad

Agamemnon sailed to Troy,
Following a naughty boy;
Paris wanted to enjoy
A holiday with flighty
Helen, Menelaus' wife,
Cause of ten years' loss of life;
Homer blamed her for the strife –
Her and Aphrodite.

Nine years later, all looked bleak;
Achilles proved a sulky Greek,
Wouldn't, in a fit of pique,
Even cross Scamander.
Agamemnon, somewhat shaken,
Quickly tried to save his bacon
And return a girl he'd taken
From his best commander.

'Late repentance isn't valid,'
Said Achilles, and he dallied
Till his friend, Patroclus, sallied
    Forth to join the battle;
By Apollo he was chivvied,
Then was killed; Achilles, livid,
Rushing out from where he'd bivvy-ed,
    Slaughtered men like cattle.

What he did then wasn't pretty:
Three times round the Trojan city,
Achilles, quite devoid of pity,
    Chased the valiant Hector,
Killed him, and – O shameful deed! –
Dragged his corpse behind his steed,
Denying him his urgent need –
    A funeral director.

Priam, father of the dead,
Came to visit him and said:
'Mercy on my ancient head!
    I will pay a ransom.'
Achilles, being much impressed,
Freely granted his request,
Thereby, as the world confessed,
    Acting very handsome.

PAUL GRIFFIN

HOMER:
The Iliad

Really it all began with Aphrodite:
Won 'Miss Olympus', bribed the judge with crumpet;
Handed him Helen, dazzling in her nightie,
    Like it or lump it.

Well, Paris liked it; Helen too, you betcher,
Not so her husband, maddened Menelaus:
'Come, all you princes, off to Troy to fetch her;
    Ships will convey us.'

But there were hitches – lack of wind for starters,
Sacrificed daughters, sickness and ill-feeling;
Hero with hero, god with goddess barters,
           Wheeling and dealing . . .

Nine years have passed, and fatal fevers follow;
Chief Agamemnon begs his seer's autopsy.
'If you'd avert the anger of Apollo,
           Give back your popsy!'

'Yes!' said Achilles. 'No!' said Agamemnon,
'Force me and I'll take yours in compensation!'
Exit Achilles, though his mates condemn non-
           Participation,

He hugs his tent, unmindful of the mighty
Conflict around him, much of it abortive,
Since of her loved ones artful Aphrodite
           'S crudely supportive;

Then there's poor Zeus, whose periodic shut-eye,
Hen-peck and chick-nip spell perpetual ill-ease . . .
Greek fortunes wane and all seems hopeless – but I
           Turn to Achilles,

Grouping his troops (though still a sworn defector),
Clothing his pal, Patroclus, in his armour,
Sending him war-wards, where he's slogged by Hector,
           Not without drama.

Anguished Achilles, dressed to kill by Thetis,
Bursts on the battle, swift to save his honour,
Rages through Trojans, dealing death – the bet is
           Hector's a goner.

Yes, this great hero, kind to kids and ladies,
Dragged through the dust, proclaims Achilles' glory;
Flames from his pyre which light the way to Hades,
           Ending the story.

MARY HOLTBY

HOMER:
The Odyssey

Odysseus, starting his journey home after beating the Trojans,
Thanks to the tempers and fusses common in gods on Olympus,
Found himself long years voyaging, landing on very strange islands,
Like that of the giant Polyphemus, vast, fierce, partially sighted,
Who earned, thanks to our hero, his full disability pension.
Then there were amorous girl friends, one in particular, Circe;
She turned his men into piglets and had to be threatened with moly,
Which made her sweetly compliant; she soon had a son by Odysseus.
After he steered past the Sirens, tied hand and foot to the mainmast,
Dodging the horrors of Scylla and the dangerous whirlpool Charybdis,
He drifted where lovely Calypso claimed seven years of his voyage.
At last upon Ithaca's sea-coast he landed; nobody knew him
Except his old hunting dog, Argus, who wagged his tail and departed.
Penelope, faithful as ever, was staunchly resisting advances
From dozens of insolent princes, and weaving a shroud for her husband,
Taking her time in the process. She now set a task for her suitors:
To string a great bow and to use it – an early form of Olympics.
Odysseus won the gold medal; none of the other aspirants
Needed, to put it politely, the return half of their tickets.
Down long years come principles: three of them, plain and disturbing:
Cunning and physical prowess will see a man through in the long run;
Beautiful girls are abundant, but tend to prove rather demanding;
Women must always be constant, but men can do just as they fancy.
Homer or Ian Fleming: it comes to the same in the long run.

PAUL GRIFFIN

HOMER:
The Odyssey

After the fall of Troy the Greeks were scattered;
Crafty Odysseus, whose wits they all relied on,
Suffered from storms, his ships mislaid and shattered,
       Thanks to Poseidon.

Wrecked on the island of a one-eyed monster,
Trapped in a cave convenient for his dinner,
Much meditation helped our hardened conster
> Dream up a winner:

Sharpening a pole, he fired the point and biffed him,
Sent him de-opticked screaming for his mummy,
Chose for each man a giant sheep to lift him
> Tied to its tummy.

Thus they escape, but, ever at the mercy
Of piqued Poseidon, tend to cut things fine-ish:
Cannibals, windbags – then a touch of Circe,
> Turning things swinish.

Grunts change to speech – the remedy is herbal –
Then off to Hades to see a seer and sound him;
Much information, visual and verbal,
> Gathers around him.

Warned of his trials, onward sails our captain:
Strapped to the mast resists seductive Sirens;
Scylla, Charybdis trust he'll soon be trapped in
> *Their* dire environs.

Vainly the vortex whirled, but Scylla craned her
Claws, to seize six; alas! that lust for plunder
Swiftly ensured the ravenous remainder
> Joined them down under.

Solo Odysseus must complete his trip, so,
Finding himself in quite a cushy billet,
Fed and caressed by amorous Calypso,
> Will he fulfil it?

See him once more committed to the water,
Wrecked once again, by fierce Poseidon harassed,
Washed to the feet of Alcinous' fair daughter,
> Rather embarrassed;

Swapping his figleaf for a suit more sightly,
Telling his host the story of his travels ...
Back home his wife weaves daily, and then nightly
        Subtly unravels,

Cheating her suitors, whose persistent misuse
Ruined the palace till its long-lost master,
Dressed like a tramp but acting like Odysseus,
        Brought them disaster –

Simply transfixed them into recognition,
Drew his great bow and ultimately floored them;
Kissed wife and son; the long years' intermission
Spelled out in detail, as I here record them
(Or in a somewhat bowdlerised edition,
        Which might have bored them).

MARY HOLTBY

HENRIK IBSEN:
A Doll's House

    Torvald Helmer was a bastard,
    And a smug young banker, too.
    On his wife he fairly plastered
    Pet-names of a fulsome hue!
    She'd once forged – to save his carcass,
    Though her husband never knew!

    Soon along comes fly-boy Krogstad,
    Threatening to blow the gaff;
    Just an importuning jobs cad –
    Wants a place on Torvald's staff! ...
    Nora pleaded, hanging holly;
    Torvald sneered: 'Don't make me laugh!'

    Sure as eggs, comes Krogstad's letter –
    HELL – DAMNATION – GUMBOILS – POX –
    To repose – why, nowhere better –
    Deep in Torvald's letter-box!

Nora, dreading he should read it,
Thought she'd better press her frocks!

Then she danced a tarantella,
To distract him – O, what guile!
Till he cried out: 'To the cellar!'
When he'd read the Krogstad File! . . .
How he blamed her and defamed her,
In an un-Christmassy style!

Soon he went for her bald-headed –
Forgers should be in the nick!
She must live apart, though wedded;
Not corrupt babes Dot and Dick! . . .
THEN – that forged note was recovered!!!
HALLELUJAH – Burn it, quick!

All she's done is now forgiven;
She is still his chickadee! . . .
Nora, now with insight riven,
Slings her wedding-ring – and key!
Then she strolls down to the station,
Leaving kids and Torvald – *FREE*!

PASCO POLGLAZE

HENRIK IBSEN:
Ghosts

FJORD FUZZ FLOORED!
HEARTBREAK LOVER IN FIRE RIDDLE

Top Oslo arson experts confessed themselves baffled last night by the towering inferno that totally destroyed the Captain Alving Orphanage within hours of its official opening.

Its founder, local Lady Bountiful Mrs Alving (51), was said to be too distressed to comment on the catastrophe that has reduced her life's mission to ashes.

Top trustee, veteran bible-basher and soul-snatcher, Pastor Manders (65), was unavailable for comment upon a report rife in this rumour-ridden little community that it was he who vetoed 'Insult to God' insurance on the orphanage.

Orphanage carpenter Jakob Engstrand (61) was reported to be so shocked by the disaster as to be unable to stand. Friends described him as too tired and emotional to comment coherently on a report that he was seen leaving the Orphanage, minutes before the flames erupted, with a bottle and a blow-lamp.

His daughter, bouncy, nubile, fun-loving Regina (17), who works at the Alving residence, is said to have the hots and no mistake for her employer's son, Osvald Alving (23), lately returned from pursuing his studies and who knows what else in Gay oo-la-la Paree. Regina, who has sentimental associations with the Alving mansion in that her mother also worked there, leaving somewhat hurriedly just before Regina's birth, is said to be upset by rumours that there may be just cause and impediment to prevent her union with handsome young Osvald.

Meanwhile, wagging tongues are whispering that the late Captain Alving's only battle-scars were sustained on the fields of Venus. Some of the symptoms of young Mr Alving's current 'indisposition' are said to be remarkably similar to those of his late lamented father's last illness.

Investigations continue into a mystery that is the universal talking-point for at least a mile in any given direction.

MARTIN FAGG

HENRIK IBSEN:
Hedda Gabler

The Coroner sums up:

The only unequivocal fact you have to go on, Members of the Jury, is that Mrs Hedda Tesman – Miss Hedda *Gabler*, I nearly said – for it is, I am sure, as the late General Gabler's splendidly spirited daughter that we shall best remember her – died of a self-inflicted bullet wound in the temple.

How to Become Ridiculously Well-Read ...

Now I must not, of course, seek to influence your verdict in any way, but I think we can dismiss at the start any question of suicide. After all, why should this brilliant and attractive young woman, the cynosure of so much admiration, destroy herself when she had everything to live for?

She had, after all, only just returned from an extended wedding tour with her beloved husband, Dr Jörgen Tesman. Dr Tesman is, I need hardly inform you, a most distinguished scholar – and what greater bliss could any newly married young wife envisage than spending the rest of her days till death did them part, locked in the company of the author of books on such topics as domestic crafts in Brabant in the Middle Ages? I have not yet myself had the privilege of perusing any of Dr Tesman's publications, but I am told that they exercise a most powerful – well-nigh hypnotic effect – on all those who open them, however briefly.

As I say, I must not pre-empt your verdict in any way, but as 'Accidental Death' is so obviously the only one that any responsible or rational body of citizens could possibly bring in on the evidence before us, the question of undue influence does not arise and I do *not*, I repeat, Members of the Jury, attempt to influence you in any way.

Judge Brack, a man ever erect and notorious for his honour, has testified to the late Mrs Tesman's playful – but now, alas, we can see, somewhat *unwise* – penchant for indoor pistol practice with the pair of handsome weapons bequeathed to her by her redoubtable father. And as the admirable Judge went on to tell us that he regarded Mrs Tesman almost as a surrogate daughter, I think we can quite properly attach great significance to their relationship, and correspondingly to his evidence.

But none at all, I fear, to the evidence of the Tesmans' servant, Berte. Hysteria (understandable on the loss of such a perfect mistress) is the kindest, indeed the only possible explanation of her wild and reeling words. Admitting that she was spying and eavesdropping on her mistress, she claims that she saw her fuelling the living-room stove with some large object and overheard her confessing that it was a child! – the child allegedly of one 'Thea' and 'Ejlert Lövborg'.

Now, apart from the fact that Mrs Tesman was plainly not reared as a stoker, it is beyond the bounds of belief that such a well brought-up young woman should have put a domestic stove – quite apart from the infant – to such a patently improper use. Dr Tesman, with a hesitance only too pardonable in his distressed condition, could not really enlighten us on this matter, but was of the opinion that what the maid saw being burnt was probably some unwanted old manuscript. So, Members of the Jury, you may dismiss from your deliberations the farrago of nonsense concocted in poor Berte's enfeebled brain.

It so happens that, by an extraordinary coincidence, a Mr Ejlert Lövborg, an author of some kind, also perished that very same afternoon as the result of a similar firearm accident on the premises of a lady known as Mademoiselle Diana – a sort of informal tea-room, I gather, where young men and women of intellectual interests engage one another in light cerebral banter. It also so happens that this gentleman had in fact visited the Tesman residence several times in the previous twenty-four hours – but what of that? So had Dr Tesman's aunt, so had Mrs Thea Elvsted, so had Judge Brack.

I have absolutely no idea whatsoever what your verdict is going to be, Members of the Jury, but would you please now retire and consider it.

Verdict: Death by Misadventure

MARTIN FAGG

HENRIK IBSEN:
The Master Builder

The Coroner sums up:

The only perplexing feature of this case, Members of the Jury, is why, when the late Mr Solness was reportedly afraid of heights and subject to acute giddiness at altitude, he should himself have gone up the ladders to place the symbolic wreath round the weathervane of his splendid new home.

Vertigo is, of course, a quite sufficient explanation of his having thereafter fallen to his death. I need hardly add that that death has robbed us of one of our most respected citizens – a man who, entirely self-taught and self-made, never aspired to the pompous appellation of architect, but was content simply to be the Master Builder of hundreds of comfy, keenly priced, all-mod-con, bijou homes, in one of which I myself cosily reside.

Not the least distressing aspect of this lamentable case is the unhinging effect it has plainly had on the two ladies who have given evidence.

I am sure we all feel for Mrs Solness, the widow of the deceased. It is understandable that her mind, in its state of shock, should have reverted to the destruction by fire of her old family home in the early years of her marriage and the subsequent death of her two small twin boys. You will recall that, in answer to my questions, she was able to talk only of nurseries, dresses, lace, jewels and dolls, and you will, I am sure, pardon the total irrelevance of evidence that I should have been obliged to construe, from other lips, as wilfully obstructive. She was clearly anxious to enlighten us about the circumstances of the tragedy but was as clearly unable to do so.

The case of the other, much younger, lady who happened to be staying with the Solnesses at the time was, if anything, even more upsetting. I may as well quell any idle speculation there may be about the reason for her presence in the Solness home at the time by saying that, though no blood relation, she obviously regarded Mr Solness as some sort of honorary uncle. And, in this regard, let him who is without a mote in his own eye cast the first beam through the greenhouse window.

At all events, when I questioned this very personable young woman, she promptly insisted, you will recall, on my addressing her not as Miss Hilde Wangel, but as Princess Hilde of Orangia. She also imposed a strain on our credulity by asserting that, just before Mr Solness fell to his death, she had commissioned him to buy her a kingdom and build her a castle – and by attributing the sole responsibility for his demise to a troll, whom, however, she was totally unable to name or identify. Miss Wangel is now undergoing treatment in the local funny – psychiatric clinic – and Members of the Jury will be reassured to know that as soon as the shrinks think her fit for discharge, she will find a friendly half-way house back to reality under my own hospitable roof-tree. Now, pray retire.

Open Verdict

MARTIN FAGG

HENRY JAMES:
The Aspern Papers

You are asking what I am doing in this Italian city that is built in such a crazy place a guy cannot hang around the sidewalks without his feet are getting very wet indeed. I will inform you why I am here. There is a guy called Jeff the Jingle, a citizen who is worth a considerable amount of dough in spite of the fact that he is dead a very long time, and who is giving me quite a belt out of the stuff he writes. Now Jeff is once the kind of smooth operator who likes to sweet-talk certain high-class broads, and, what is more, likes to put this and plenty of other stuff on paper. To me this seems like a dangerous move but I am not Jeff the Jingle so let it pass. It turns out that one of these broads, Bordereau by name, is still alive in a run-down joint in this Italian city I am mentioning, and has the low-down on Jeff the Jingle stashed away somewhere. That is one bundle of papers I would like to take a peek at but the Bordereau broad is one suspicious old dame and don't see no one.

Now this Judy lives in the joint with her niece who is no big deal to look at. In fact, the general view is that both Bordereau broads are a crazy pair of dolls, and it does not take a lot of education to see that the old Judy is turning the niece, little Miss Tina, into a first-class sucker, so I think maybe I can make some progress by giving the young doll the big eyes.

For a very long time I do not even mention Jeff the Jingle but I am doing nicely with little Miss Tina and even get myself a rat-hole in the old Judy's joint. I figure that if I can hang on she is going to die pretty soon and Little Miss Tina is giving me no trouble over fingering Jeff the Jingle's papers. Well, the old Judy does not die but one day she shows me Jeff's kisser on a little picture her old man knocked out and I am surprised to learn that she is keen to make a few potatoes on a deal. I think that perhaps I am close to getting what I want so I let out to Little Miss Tina the news that I am a big fan of Jeff the Jingle. She does not take this too well, however, and makes for the door at considerable speed leaving me with the thought that I have blown it.

This is not so, though, because suddenly the old Judy gets sick and I find I am able to take a snoop about the place at night. In fact, I am creeping up to this classy looking bureau that looks full of promise to me when the old Judy pops out of a door, gives me a lot of not very nice lip and takes a back-dive into the arms of Little Miss

Tina. This, I am thinking, is a good time to quit and so that is what I do.

I leave the Bordereau broads to it for a considerable spell, and when I return Little Miss Tina gives me to understand that the old Judy has bought it while I am away. She also tells me I can have Jeff the Jingle's papers, the snag being I have to get hitched to her. I have already said that she is no big deal to look at so it is quite natural for my eyes to pop a certain degree at this information. Unfortunately, Little Miss Tina takes this to be a bad sign.

The next day I see her again and I think to myself maybe she is a better looker than I am at first believing but it is just now that she tells me she has had a blaze-up with Jeff the Jingle's papers. I know this to be the way some dames behave but I find that I do not like what I am hearing. I come away with nothing but the little picture and, I tell you, every time I see Jeff the Jingle's kisser staring down at me from my wall it is giving me the creeps.

N.J.WARBURTON

HENRY JAMES:
The Bostonians

He's done it again! Our guess is that's what you'll be saying to yourself when you start reading Henry James's latest *exposé* of upper-crust Boston.

It's all there. The grand houses. The grand manners. The to-and-fro of ideas. The secret passions of men and women. Henry James knows his Boston, and he brings it alive for the reader as no other novelist can.

But there's another Boston, too. Beneath the smart dinner-parties and the dignified talk lurks a sinister threat. The Women's Movement, innocent and high-minded as it looks, conceals dark motives and dubious characters. Mrs Birdseye, preaching sedition. Olive Chancellor, nursing unnatural desires. And a whole host of 'short-haired women and long-haired men'.

It's strong meat. But it's a story the author insists must be told. And at the heart of it all is the beautiful Verena Tarrant. Will she succumb to Olive Chancellor or will the dashing, dispossessed Southerner Basil Ransom save her?

Romance, mystery, suspense, intrigue. It's a formula that can't fail. But in the hands of a writer like James it's more than a formula. It's a piece of tip-top entertainment that will grip you like a vice.

BASIL RANSOME-DAVIES

HENRY JAMES:
Daisy Miller

Daisy, Daisy,
Innocent Yank – or broad?
In Rome at play she
Acts of her own accord,
Men friends question her intentions
As she flouts high-class conventions,
But a mosquito
Strikes a fatal blow,
And her reputation's restored.

V. ERNEST COX

HENRY JAMES:
The Turn of the Screw

She was poor but she was earnest,
And she had to earn her keep;
So she went down into Essex,
Teaching gentry on the cheap.

Little Miles and little Flora,
Lovely kiddies, so well bred,
Only had one disadvantage –
They were haunted by the dead.

Peter Quint and grim Miss Jessel –
She who taught the kids before –
Should have rested in their coffins,
But they yearned to live some more.

Grisly Peter glared through windows,
Jessel sobbed upon the stair,
And it seemed the kids could see them,
Simply loved to have them there.

And the snag our poor girl suffered
Was she saw the ghosts as well;
No one else could ever see them
But the kids, who wouldn't tell.

So nobody could believe her,
Tended just to put her down.
Flora, lucky, got a fever
And was taken safe to town.

While our heroine faced Peter,
Got him out of Miles's head,
But the shock was too much for him –
Exorcised, poor Miles dropped dead.

It's the same the whole world over,
You can't win, with ghost or hex.
People who don't see what you see
Put it down to good old sex.

PHYLLIS PARKER

JEROME K. JEROME:
Three Men in a Boat

(*A page from* Old Barker's Book of Practical Dogs)

MONTMORENCY

Oh, Montmorency is a dog, a terrier at that,
A fox one, though in London all he chases is a cat,
And failing that and dog-fights, then his one idea of fun
Is to make himself a nuisance and to trip up everyone.

He had a simply splendid time when Harris, George
   and J.
Were packing up the hamper for their river holiday.
He sat upon the saucers and he slobbered at the ham,
Squashed half the pies and bit the spoons and walked into
   the jam.

But life with three men in a boat – what was the point of
   that?
No dogs to fight, no cats to chase, he found things very
   flat;
Though when they thought to use up bits and make an
   Irish stew,
He went and brought a water-rat for them to put in too.

It was at Marlow, Montmorency met his Waterloo,
He spied a quite enormous Tom at which he simply flew.
But big black Tom just turned around and looked the way
   cats do,
All calm and unconcerned, and said: 'What can I do for
   you?'

And Montmorency, shame-faced, dropped his tail in its
   groove
And muttered: 'Nothing, thank you', and then thought it
   best to move.
The only other *contretemps* that Monty did not settle
Was with a nasty spiteful, spitting, hissing, boiling kettle.

To look at Montmorency, you would think an angel had
Come down to earth in doggy shape. His soulful eyes are
  sad
And there is such a 'What-a-wicked-world-this-is-and-
  how-
I-wish-I-could-do-something-for-it' look upon his brow.

Yet what this most disreputable dog likes best of all
Is collecting up a gang of curs and setting up a brawl,
A seething mass of dogs who snap and yap for all they're
  worth,
So – so much for the notion he's an angel come to earth.

                                        JOYCE JOHNSON

JAMES JOYCE:
Finnegan's Wake

Finnegan's Wake
Is one long spelling mistake
With not a lot
Of plot.

Its central theme,
Revealed through H. C. Earwicker's dream,
Is the cyclical pattern of fall and resurrection,
But except for a few good puns it's not worth close
  inspection.

                                        V. ERNEST COX

JAMES JOYCE:
Ulysses

*Bloom is in the bedroom of Number 7 Eccles Street removing
his socks before retiring for the night. He is surprised to see
the head of Eamonn Andrews appear from beneath the bed.*

EAMONN: Leopold Bloom, small-time advertising man, wanderer,
cuckold, Jew, would-be poet and father to sons – This Is
Your Life!
[*Music. A bemused Bloom is ushered into a taxi and thence
to a studio.*]

EAMONN: Heh heh! Well, Leopold, cast your mind back, if you will, to
that fateful morning of 16th June, 1904, and this voice . . .

MOLLY [*sleepily, from behind some curtains*]: Mn.

BLOOM: Molly!

EAMONN: Yes indeed! The wife you left behind in bed. Singer,
temptress, mistress to a multitude – Mrs Molly Bloom!
[*Molly's bed is wheeled janglingly in.*]

EAMONN: That must've been quite a day for Leopold here, Molly.

MOLLY [*taking a deep breath*]: . . . yes because he never did a thing
like that before as ask to get his breakfast in bed with a
couple of eggs since 'The City Arms Hotel' when he used
to be . . .

EAMONN [*wheeling her hurriedly aside*]: Heh heh! Yes, I'm sure. Well,
if you remember, Leo, later on that morning you had an
important appointment to keep. Does this voice mean
anything to you?
[*Silence*]

BLOOM: What voice?

EAMONN: What voice indeed! You thought you'd seen the last of him
back in that cemetery in Dublin but here, specially to greet
you, is . . .

BLOOM: Paddy Dignam! I don't believe it!
[*Paddy is carried on. Bloom embraces him and helps him to
a seat.*]

EAMONN: And so you continued to wander aimlessly through the
Dublin streets little realising that, incredible though it
may seem, a young man you hardly knew was doing exactly
the same thing . . .

STEPHEN [*from behind the curtain*]: Ineluctable modality of the
visible . . .

BLOOM: What?

EAMONN: You weren't to know it then but you were destined to meet
that young man later that very same night in a brothel in
Nighttown. Come in, Stephen Dedalus!
[*Bloom tearfully greets Stephen who immediately leaves the
studio, the building and subsequently the country. Before the
curtains can close Bella Cohen and two whores enter to greet
Bloom affectionately and exchange whispered notes with
Molly.*]

N. J. WARBURTON

FRANZ KAFKA:
Metamorphosis

Well, I stayed up yesterday evenin'
With mah train times neatly filed;
Then I set mah clock to early
And man, mah dreams was wild.

Yeah, I woke up early this mornin'
And I opened up mah eyes –
I found I was a beetle,
Metamorphosised!

(*Chorus:*)
Mah world's turned upside down.
I got those b-b-b-bedsitter blues –
(*Bedsitter, bed, bedsitter*) –
Sure is grey all over town
With the b-b-b-bedsitter blues!

Hey, mah paw's been chuckin' apples
And one landed in mah back,
But sis is busy workin'
And that's a natural fact.

Mah mom ain't got no asthma
And they're bringin' home the loot.
Yeah, and I stopped feelin' hungry –
Especially for fruit!

> (*Chorus:*)
> Mah world's turned upside down.
> I got those b-b-b-bedsitter blues –
> (*Bedsitter, bed, bedsitter*) –
> Sure is grey all over town
> With the b-b-b-bedsitter blues!

Well, they done got in some lodgers,
Each with his coat and beard;
Mah sis sure plays that fiddle sweet
But the tenants, they look *weird*.

So I went out early this evenin'
With a tear inside mah eye –
Hey, how come they turn upon me?
I'll love them till I die . . .

> (*Chorus:*)
> Mah world's turned upside down.
> I got those b-b-b-bedsitter blues –
> (*Bedsitter, bed, bedsitter*) –
> Sure is grey all over town
> With the b-b-b-bedsitter blue-ue-ue-ues!

BILL GREENWELL, JOE EWART, ANNIE SYMONS

FRANZ KAFKA:
The Trial

Busted, locked away,
Dude named K. The rap is crap –
Metaphor, they say.

But who's against whom?
We assume it's Fate and State,
Ending in Man's doom.

Is this how Life goes –
Only lows? Are highs such lies –
Or this book a pose?

TIM HOPKINS

CHARLES KINGSLEY:
The Water Babies

This tells of Tom the Sweep and Grimes,
His master; but one must suppose
That children of Victorian times
Were used to chunks of pious prose.

But to the story. Let's proceed.
Down the wrong chimney Tom has come
Into another world indeed,
A clean white bedroom. Tom is dumb.

He gazes in amazement at
A little girl in bed, asleep.
But in the mirror – who is that?
A nasty, dirty chimney-sweep!

He runs off, scared he may be caught.
Never such a chase was seen!
In Tom's head though, there's but one thought –
'I must be clean, I must be clean!'

And clean he is, washed by a brook –
As clean as you, or cleaner, maybe.
His skin is white as white – and look!
Tom has become a water baby!

He plays about and learns a lot;
But if he plays too many tricks
That are unkind, he finds he's got
A rash of horrid prickly pricks.

After more sermons (why, oh why?)
Tom duly sees, when duly chid,
Dame Doasyouwouldbedoneby
Is Dame Bedonebyasyoudid.

But when the action's not delayed,
It's fun with Tom all clean and new.
If only Kingsley could have made
A clean sweep of his sermons too!

JOYCE JOHNSON

RUDYARD KIPLING:
The Jungle Book

Mother Wolf speaks:
'Mowgli the man cub came to me, looked up at me, and smiled,
A naked babe, quite unafraid, alone and in the wild.
He may not be blood of my blood, nor yet bone of my bone,
But came to me for comfort, and I love him like my own.'

Shere Khan, the Tiger, speaks:
'That man cub is my due, and it is great Shere Khan who speaks.
I'll bide my time, if bide I must, for many days and weeks.
But mine he is and any Wolf that balks me will be sorry,
For I'm Shere Khan the Terrible who always gets his quarry!'

Akela, Leader of the Wolf Pack, speaks:

'Look well, O Wolves – What have the Free to do with those
    not Free?
I shall not live for ever, and then who will follow me?
Look well upon this Mowgli now – who speaks for this cub, who?'
And old Baloo, the sleepy Bear, rose up and growled: 'I do.'

Baloo, the Bear, continues:

'I'll teach this little man cub, he'll learn quickly while he's young.
He'll learn the Wood and Water Laws, the Jungle Law and Tongue.
I'll teach him all the Master-Words, the Stranger's Hunting
    Call,
For Jungle Law must be obeyed, and he must learn it *all*.'

Bagheera, the Black Panther, speaks:

'And I, Bagheera, I tell you to kill a cub is shame.
The Pack can have the bull I killed if you will add my name.
Baloo can do the brain work, but I'll teach him how to climb
And how to hunt and whom to kill. He may teach *us* in time.'

Mowgli speaks:

'And so, of all the animals, Bagheera and Baloo
Were chief among the Jungle Folk who taught me what to do.
And Chil the Kite and Mang the Bat and Kaa the Snake and others,
With prickly Ikki Porcupine, I counted as my Brothers.
Akela and Grey Brother helped me do old Shere Khan in,
And now, upon the Council Rock, we have his Tiger skin.'

JOYCE JOHNSON

RUDYARD KIPLING:
The Just So Stories

But just so – what? Just so we'd know the
               Why and When and How
The animals have come to look the way that
               they do now,
The 'scrutiating Camel with his most Cam-
               eelious Hump,
And Old Man Kangaroo with legs made for a
               ten-foot jump.

We learn why the Rhinoceros has such a
                                wrinkly skin,
It used to button underneath – else, how
                                did he get in?
And then about the Elephant whose curt-
                                iosity
Led to a nose-pull and the cry: 'Led go!
                                You're hurtig be!'

And did you know the Armadillo is a kind
                                of mix
Of Slow-and-Solid Tortoise and a Hedgehog
                                full of Pricks?
And that the Whale got his throat because
                                he nearly ate
A Sailor with Suspenders (two) which you
                                must *not* forget.

And then there is the Alphabet – we see
                                how that was made,
Which gives rise to a point to which
                                attention should be paid –
If Tegumai and Tiffimai had not been
                                just so smitten,
When making all those picture words, would
                                this book have been written?

                                            JOYCE JOHNSON

RUDYARD KIPLING:
Kim

Kim
Wasn't dim,
But he was a bit of a yah-boo
Until he learnt the Game from a Babu.

He had played games before
In Lahore;
A boy who could fool a horse-trader working for the Raj
Could manage international espionage.

No, Kim was no fool,
Even after he'd been to school;
But he found the Game had other players
In the Himalayas.

He came to realise
That, despite the excitements of Russian spies,
For sheer drama
There was nothing like a lama.

PAUL GRIFFIN

RUDYARD KIPLING:
Stalky & Co.

Where Stalky and M'Turk and the jester, Beetle, lurk,
Dirty doings are a pretty safe prediction.
Their pranks can leave no doubts that they're quite the worst of louts
To be given heroes' roles in schoolboy fiction.

They excel in unfair fight, make their masters quake with fright,
And cry: 'I gloat!', when triumph crowns a trick.
They let a dead cat rot in an undetected spot
And the odour makes the college pretty sick.

They covet – that means 'steal' – and beat fags until they squeal,
And they like to go a-boozing out of bounds.
There's no one at the coll. who can even half-control
These anarchic and sadistic little hounds.

But before the story ends, Stalky grows up and defends
The Raj, with all his inbred style and class.
Dare we hope some Frontier foe will plug the so-and-so,
With a well-aimed bullet up the Khyber Pass?

PETER VEALE

D. H. LAWRENCE:
Lady Chatterley's Lover

Smart girls make passes
At the working classes.

WENDY COPE

D. H. LAWRENCE:
Lady Chatterley's Lover

'One had had one's doubts about Connie, of course.
Something a little, well, excitable about her from the start. And then
there was my little handicap – not the kind of thing a chap likes to
dwell on, but it may have contributed. To her indefinable stirrings,
I mean. The gamekeeper chappie couldn't believe his luck – she just
chucked herself at him. Fine-looking fellow, no doubt about that.
Deucedly good pheasant plucker too. But not much up here – he was
simply her tool. Her language started to go downhill – that was my
first inkling. Words I shouldn't care to repeat served up, cool as you
like, over the devilled kidneys. Soon rubs off, doesn't it? The influence
of the labouring classes, I mean. Things ended acrimoniously – she
had the cheek to accuse me of cant. At least I think she said cant . . .'

PETER NORMAN

D. H. LAWRENCE:
Sons and Lovers

All I want is a womb somewhere,
Far away from the world's compare,
So warm, so snug, such care,
Oh, wouldn't it be muvverly?
No more coarseness from uncouth Pa,
No more girl-friends to upstage Ma,
In my small world I'd star,
Oh, wouldn't it be muvverly?
O, so muvverly Freud could write a-blooming-nother tome,
I'd be happy in my cosy, Oedipally ideal home.
All I want is a place to curl,
More secure than a duke or earl,
M. Klein you are a pearl,
Oh, wouldn't it be muvverly,
Muvverly, muvverly?

All I want is a place to thrive,
Grub laid on and a chance to skive,
Drone-like in my queen's hive,
Oh, wouldn't it be muvverly?
No more rough boys to laugh and stare,
No more smut talked of pubic hair,
No self-abuse, I swear,
Oh, wouldn't it be muvverly?
Oh, so muvverly I'd survive a-blooming-nother-war,
Safe inside the only Mum who isn't a worthless whore.
All I want is a place to hide,
No more worries and no more pride,
With my eternal bride,
Oh, wouldn't it be muvverly,
Muvverly, muvverly?

TIM HOPKINS

LAURIE LEE:
Cider with Rosie

Writ in evocative prose,
Cider with Rose
Is the memoirs of a Cotswold kid,
What he saw, felt and did.

It's like a chapter from *The Archers*
With arrivals and departures,
But reads much better, for
Its simile and metaphor
Lift it from the rough
Of other rural stuff.

Cutting pretty-pretty –
Here's the nitty-gritty:

Laurie Lee (and family)
Move to Slad (minus Dad),
Fevered head (shares Mom's bed),
Then recovers (sleeps with bruvvers),
Village school (teachers rule),
Grannies two (oh, funny duo),
Revelations ('bout relations),
Homicide (and suicide),
Visit to Weston (Sunday best on),
Rose and cider (Loll's beside her),
Attempted rape (just a jape!),
Squire's demise (village dies).

V. ERNEST COX

HERMAN MELVILLE:
Moby-Dick

A captain with an *idée fixe*
Chased a whale for weeks and weeks,
All because it ate his limb:
That's the thing that bothered him.

In the end, with scarce a scratch,
The whale it won – game, set and match.
And though it seems a bit bizarre
The whale was white – an odd *bête noire*.

W.S.BROWNLIE

ARTHUR MILLER:
The Crucible

Lust alight and bibles busy,
Teenage tartlets in a tizzy;
Aged crone and damsel dewy –
Who is witch and which is hooey?
Church and courtroom atmospherics
Manufacture mass hysterics;
Pride and perjury pervade,
Saints and slags are martyrs made . . .

Artful Abigail loves Proctor,
Who'd incautiously unfrocked her;
She, while various victims cop it,
Snares his wife with pinpricked poppet,
Drives him to a false confession
Of demoniac possession.
Proctor's ultimate repentance
Seals the pious judge's sentence,
So he goes, in fine furore,
Most reluctantly to glory.

This I make my sole indictment:
There is far too much excitement.
Confidence entirely ebbs
In the opium of the plebs.

MARY HOLTBY

A. A. MILNE:
The House at Pooh Corner

A Hum of Pooh called
SPECIAL PLACES

Rumpty Tumpty Rumpty Tum
Here are the places where we come,
     The Six Pine Trees and such.
There's MR SANDERS, which is where
I live, and I am Pooh the Bear.
I hope I go on living there.
     I like it very much.

There's Piglet's House (he lives here too)
Next to TRESPASSERS W.
     (That is his grandpa's name.)
The Bee Tree, that was full of bees,
And Eeyore's House of sticks – all these
We built, so that he wouldn't freeze –
     He grumbled all the same.

There's Rabbit's Hole, where I got stuck,
And Owl's House where Piglet's pluck
     Rose nobly to our need.
He bravely did as he was bid
And squoze himself right through the lid
Of LETTERS ONLY – Oh, he did
     A Very Splendid Deed.

Another of our Special Places
Is Poohstick Bridge, where we run races
     And watch whose Poohstick comes.
This Hum is getting rather long,
Is it a Hum – or more a song?
Some Hums go right and some go wrong,
     You can never tell with Hums.

JOYCE JOHNSON

A. A. MILNE:
Winnie the Pooh

A Hum by Pooh
FOR CHRISTOPHER ROBIN

There's been a Hum about Piglet,
There's been a Hum about Pooh,
But this is an Extra Special Hum
For this is a Hum about you.

Who helped pretend I was a cloud?
When I was wedged, who did me proud
And brought a book and read aloud?
    Why, Christopher Robin, of course.

Who, when he saw those paw-marks, knew
Why there was one and then were two –
Not Woozles – but a Foolish Pooh
    And Piglet both after a Wizzle?

Who laughed to see a Heffalump,
Or Hoffalump or Hellerump,
Biff-bang its head an awful thump,
    And found out it was only me?

Who knew the Piglet wasn't Roo,
And sailed the good ship *Brain of Pooh*,
And led an Expotition to
    The Pole and said Pooh it was found it?

Who gave a Party just for me,
And a case with pencils marked 'H B'
For 'Helping Bear' – that's clever – See?
    Why, Christopher Robin, that's who.

Who says, when I go off and do
A silly stupid thing: 'Oh, Pooh!'
And then: 'Oh, Bear, I *do* love you!'
          By now, you can probably guess.

                    JOYCE JOHNSON

A. A. MILNE:
Winnie the Pooh

FIRST VOICE: Time has passed. The sun shines on the Hundred Acre
          Wood, where wise Mr Wol, past hunting, sits blear-eyed
          behind his bell-pull, dreaming of . . .

MR WOL: . . . the crustimony proceedcake.

FIRST VOICE: Old Rabbit sees not so fine in the grass-green morning,
          as he bustles about his burrowing ways, nodding to the
          bear who hums in the honey-clogged sun under the name
          of SANDERS.

POOH: Three cheers for Pooh!
          But what *did* I do?
          It's time for a little Something.

FIRST VOICE: Day. It is cloudy over the dells and dingles, where
          crazed Eeyore stands gloomy in the hoof-high marsh. A
          cloud bursts musically over the North Pole, where Piglet,
          entirely surrounded by Time, waits for Christopher Robin
          to stump wellington-booted across the flooding years.

PIGLET: Where are you, Christopher Robin? Leading Expotitions
          to hunt Heffalumps? Fighting with Kings, and Queens
          and Factors? It's been a long time; and it's raining.

CHRISTOPHER ROBIN: The Woozles got me long ago, while I was
          having my bath.

MRS KANGA: Go to bed, Piglet . . .

FIRST VOICE: . . . says grandmotherly Mrs Kanga.

MRS KANGA: And you too, Roo.

ROO: But I've only just got up! . . .

FIRST VOICE: . . . squeaks lazy Roo, dabbling in the sun-long streams
          below the Six Pine Trees, where Tigger had bounced
          rheumatically on two of Rabbit's friends and relations.
          Old Christopher Robin jumps in his far-off sleep,
          ransacking the blinded nurseries of his dreams.

CHRISTOPHER ROBIN: Silly old Tigger! Mr Shepard will draw two
more.

FIRST VOICE: But they wait in vain for lost Mr Shepard and lost Mr
Milne. Pooh's cupboard is bare, Eeyore's house is down
and a mist is creeping over the Forest. Mr Wol is asleep
again, dreaming of . . .

MR WOL: . . . Planning Permission.

FIRST VOICE: Time has passed.

PAUL GRIFFIN

JOHN MILTON:
Paradise Lost

When an angel's flung from Heaven
    On to burning clay,
He may surely be forgiven
    If he wishes not to stay,
And regrets his lost ambition;
Seraphs sentenced to perdition
    Tend to act that way.

But the sulky fits pass over
    And the tantrums fade;
Decent angels soon recover,
    Grit their teeth, and make the grade;
Only those who crave attention
(Satan is the one I'd mention)
    Turn out renegade.

Sad it was that to our planet
    Satan spread his wings,
Tempted Eve with pomegranate,
    Flattered her with whisperings;
Though the Lord had said: 'Leave this 'un!'
Naughty Eve refused to listen,
    Made a mess of things.

Angels turned her out of Eden,
    Nor could Adam stay;
So this couple, in their greed 'n'
    Wicked failure to obey,
Found they'd lost each lovely acre,
And, repentant, had to take a
    Solitary way.

PAUL GRIFFIN

IRIS MURDOCH:
A Severed Head

A Severed Head – a splendid title this!
The plot, no doubt, concerns decapitation.
The reader, on this same hypothesis,
Picks up the book with keen anticipation.

Martin, it seems, a social diplomat,
Simply adores Antonia, his wife,
But doesn't tell his mistress, Georgie, that!
(He hankers for the peaceful sort of life.)

Antonia's in love with Palmer. He
With sister Honor's rather more than chummy!
Incest? Just semi-incest for, you see,
They'd different dads, albeit the self-same mummy.

'And when, pray, does the butchery begin?'
The baffled reader plaintively inquires.
Patience, my friend, the book is fairly thin –
Hearken to what eventually transpires.

Martin meets Honor now and she produces
A Japanese *samurai* sword and then,
After a martial demonstration, pushes
It, bloodless, back into its sheath again.

The nicely written balderdash goes on –
Antonia has married Martin's brother –
Palmer and Georgie to the States have gone –
Martin and Honor now love one another!

A severed head? A taboo symbol merely.
The avid reader, now completely choked,
Tossing the book aside, remarks severely:
'The Trade Descriptions Act should be invoked!'

T. L. McCARTHY

VLADIMIR NABOKOV:
Lolita

What the Papers Said:

**LONELY LECTURER LODGES WITH
LOVELORN LADY**

**LASCIVIOUS LODGER LUSTS AFTER LANDLADY'S
LISPING LITTLE LASS**

LECHEROUS LECTURER WEDS LANDLADY

**LUCKLESS LANDLADY LOSES LIFE – LODGER LEFT TO LOOK
AFTER LOLITA**

**LIVELY LOLITA LOVES LICKING LOLLIPOPS
LEWDLY!**

**LUCKY LECTURER'S ILLICIT LOVE-LIFE AS LUBRICIOUS
LOLITA'S LIVE-IN LOVER**

**LICENTIOUS LIBERTIES LAND LINGUIST IN LAW
COURT**

LOQUACIOUS LOGOPHILE LOCKED UP FOR LIFE!

PETER NORMAN

VLADIMIR NABOKOV:
Lolita

Pert, pubescent child,
Is defiled by perve with nerve,
Till Quilty gets wild ...

TIM HOPKINS

GEORGE ORWELL:
Animal Farm

The animals stage a *coup d'état*,
    Hurrah! Hurrah!
And from the farm all humans bar,
    Hurrah! Hurrah!
The literate pigs assume control,
Dictating every beast's new role,
And they change the name from
'Manor' to 'Animal Farm'.

United in one beastlyhood,
    Hurrah! Hurrah!
They chant their maxim: 'Four legs good',
    Hurrah! Hurrah!
Then Snowball and Napoleon clash –
Snowball is forced to make a dash,
And his name becomes mud
Down on the 'Animal Farm'.

Equality slips out the door,
    Ta-ta! Ta-ta!
The tyranny's worse than before,
    By far! By far!
Dissident beasts are made scapegoats,
Napoleon's dogs rip out their throats,
O the rules are changing
Down on the 'Animal Farm'.

The pigs become the new *élite*,
    Ha-ha! Ha-ha!
And start to walk on just two feet,
    Bizarre! Bizarre!
Power and corruption intertwine,
The pigs who hog it become rotten swine,
And the name's changed back to
'Manor' from 'Animal Farm'.

V. ERNEST COX

GEORGE ORWELL:
1984

In the nightmare future time, when from each wall
Giant posters of Big Brother sternly frown,
And the truth is written backwards in a scrawl,
And the values and the facts are upside down,
There exists one Winston Smith, a lowly clerk
In the Ministry of Truth (i.e. of Lies),
Which exists to keep the people in the dark,
And to print the kind of news that mystifies.
Now inside this middle-aged and gin-soaked weed,
Just a past-it sort of average sensual man,
Lives a passionate, though obsolescent, need
To find freedom, love and justice if he can.
But it's all a futile gesture in the end,
To oppose the domination of the State,
What with Thought Police and O'Brien – the phoney friend –
And the telescreens and rats, and endless Hate.
So when Winston's been detected, tricked and caught,
When he's suffered and betrayed and sold his soul,
He's consigned, like all unpersons of his sort,
To the bottomless, engulfing Memory Hole.
It's a pessimistic novel, bleak and sad.
It depicts a world eternally at war.
It shows mankind crushed and hopeless. Aren't you glad
You never lived through 1984?

BASIL RANSOME-DAVIES

HAROLD PINTER:
The Caretaker

ACT I

Enter DAVIES. *He pauses. He looks around.*
[*Silence*]
[*Enter* ASTON. *He sees* DAVIES. *He is about to speak but pauses.*]
ASTON: Sorry?
[*Slight pause*]

DAVIES: What?
ASTON: Were you going to –
[Pause]
DAVIES: What? [Beat] Speak?
ASTON: Yes. [Fairly long pause] Were you?
DAVIES [not quite immediately]: No.
[Enter MICK. He pauses. He walks slowly to DAVIES.]
[Slight pause]
MICK: Hallo, who's this, then?

CURTAIN

ACT II

As before. DAVIES looks at MICK. He hesitates.
DAVIES: Jenkins.
[Pause which looks like becoming a silence but stops just short]
MICK: Oh, yes?
DAVIES: I can't wait around here all day, you know, I've got to get to Sidcup.
[Silence]
MICK [menacing]: Sidcup? Did you say Sidcup? [He waits] Don't you think you can come in here and just go on about Sidcup. [Slightly longish pause] Not if you know what's good for you.
ASTON: Someone told me what was good for me once. [Extended but not quite a long pause] It wasn't very nice.
[Short silence]

CURTAIN

ACT III

Two weeks later.
[Pause followed by a silence.]
DAVIES: It's about time you did something.
[Pause somewhere between a slight pause and a longish silence]
ASTON: What?
DAVIES: About those people. [Beat] Next door.
[Enter MICK. He looks at ASTON. ASTON leaves. A lull.]
MICK: I thought I told you. [After a sustained and threatening look] About Sidcup.

DAVIES [*He is about to pause but interrupts himself*]: I can't go to Sidcup
in these shoes.
[*Two beats*]
MICK: Oh, no?
DAVIES: Not yet.
[*Slight pause merging into a silence*]

CURTAIN

N.J.WARBURTON

PHILIP ROTH:
Portnoy's Complaint

Oh, what becomes of Jewish boys
Eclipsed by Jewish mommas?
Unlike us well-adjusted goys,
They must take on all comers.
If gorgeous *shikses* won't comply
With their priapic urges,
They'll come all by themselves in sly,
Auto-erotic splurges.
Poor Alex Portnoy gets the guilt,
But not the gingerbread;
What makes him droop, what makes him wilt,
What makes him fail in bed?
Psycho-medicine postulates
One theory or another,
But in the words of Norman Bates:
'A boy's best friend's his mother.'

BASIL RANSOME-DAVIES

WILLIAM SHAKESPEARE:
Antony and Cleopatra

Antony and comely Cleo
Float upon the River Nile,
Quaffing wine and such, *con brio*,
Banqueting, Egyptian style.

Tony loves those royal kisses,
Far – so far – from home sweet home;
When suddenly he hears his missus
Has gone and snuffed it back in Rome.

Home he goes, weds Caesar's sister:
Caesar's glad, but Tony burns
For his Cleo (how he's missed her!),
Back to Egypt now returns.

Next we have a frightful battle:
Tony flees, is fast pursued
By Caesar, crowing: 'Maybe that'll
End for good our flaming feud!'

When he hears that his adored
Cleo is reported dead,
Tony falls upon his sword,
But it seems he's been misled.

Still she lives! and he – poor geezer!
Joins her at his final gasp.
But Cleo won't live under Caesar,
And ends it, aided by an asp.

RON RUBIN

WILLIAM SHAKESPEARE:
As You Like It

To Arden! To Arden, ere arteries harden,
    The forest of drop-outs, the playground of youth!
Where Dukes duck their duties for natural beauties,
    And silver-haired rustics enunciate truth;

Where straying princesses change names and addresses,
    And twinkling transvestites test foresters' suits,
Where instant conversion assures the dispersion,
    To marriage or monkhood, of brotherly brutes.

From Arden, from Arden, with partner and pardon,
    The wrestler, the jester, the lord and the lout –
They stream from the wilderness back to the garden,
    And leave the philosopher working it out.

MARY HOLTBY

WILLIAM SHAKESPEARE:
Hamlet

Hamlet saw a ghost, whose tale
Of lust and murder turned him pale;
Ghost dissolved when dawn grew dewy . . .
(Question is – was Hamlet screwy?)

Hamlet loved Ophelia, who
Turned him down when told to do;
Shambles he who once was natty . . .
(Question is – was Hamlet batty?)

Hamlet staged his father's end,
Guilty uncle's consort penned,
Blamed for choosing sex, not *suttee* . . .
(Question is – was Hamlet nutty?)

Hamlet killed his lady's pa;
Sent to England, gone too far;
Copy-book was getting blotty . . .
(Question is – was Hamlet potty?)

Hamlet, back in Denmark, found
Poor Ophelia madly drowned;
Wished he too pushed up the daisy . . .
(Question is – was Hamlet crazy?)

Hamlet fenced with furious brother,
Fatally they struck each other;
Ma drank poison, went all droopy . . .
(Question is – was Hamlet loopy?)

Hamlet with envenomed sword,
Finally slew Uncle Claude,
Then gave up the ghost and cried:
'Now I can't be certified!'

MARY HOLTBY

WILLIAM SHAKESPEARE:
Henry V

Now Hal is king, his past outgrown,
Dying Falstaff's left alone.
His nose-glow fades, his whiskers tickly
On the breast of Mistress Quickly.
Prelates plot – their own finance
To hide from Hal by war with France.
The French king's heir now sends a present
With wrappings nice, but thoughts unpleasant.
Says Hal: 'The Dauphin is a menace,
Sending me this gift of tennis
Balls.' He cries: 'By Salic Law
I've every right to go to war.
So now I will set sail for France,
And kick the Dauphin's smarty-pants.'

He first invades the Norman beaches,
Practising on Harfleur breaches.
Now bear in mind the sneer re tennis
(From that regal Gallic menace).
Ironically, the end is fought
On the field of Agincourt!
Sounds not of rackets, but of tuckets,
Knights' heads cased in battle buckets.
The French, with plumes lent by their aunts,
And natty wrought-iron underpants,

Far outnumber their opponents,
Who put their faith in stout components
Made with skill in English forges,
And bravery to match St George's.
The firing-power of English bowmen
Tops crank and bolt of Frenchy slow-men.
Unhorsed knights are loudly crashing –
Sounds of yeomen, French bonce-bashing;
Loosening their proud incisors;
Jamming down their super-visors.
Judged with care – the right amount,
Each knight is laid out '*pour le comte*'.
But then the French knights who can ride
Sink to baggage-boyicide.

The battle's o'er, the French have lost,
And men from both sides count the cost.
'You can't be serious,' Dauphin cries –
Tears are welling in his eyes.
Thus the fallen princeling winges,
Armour rusting at the hinges;
He who reeks of Chanel 5,
Deciding that to stay alive
He should concede the war is won
By him who rules o'er Channel One.
'*C'est la guerre*,' consoles the nation.
(Which means each Frenchman knows his station.)

The King returns to City cheering
With, no doubt, hogsheads of beering.
But soon, he's back again in France
For talks on peace, and on romance.
'Game, set – and match, my blushing Katy –
The place is mine, so let's get matey.'
(Katharine's the French Princess
With *doubles entendres* to caress.)

And so, with phrase-book in one hand,
Our Hal o'ercomes that foreign land.

A.P.COX

WILLIAM SHAKESPEARE:
Henry V

A LOAD OF FRENCH BALLS!

Newly crowned King Henry has just been presented with a gift. A couple of smooth-talking yes-men from the French Court delivered it yesterday. The gift, from the limp-wristed Dauphin, turned out to be a load of balls! Tennis balls, to be exact. Perhaps now the King will join the Archbishop of Canterbury and the Sun in calling for the Frogs to be put firmly in their place . . .

WHAT A GREY DAY!

What a grey day yesterday turned out to be for Sir Thomas Grey and his friends, Scroop and Cambridge. All ready to join our boys in the great fight for freedom across the Channel, the three Lords were in for a nasty shock as King Hal stepped up to demand the death penalty! Following Sun reports earlier in the week that the three had been spotted in gay bars, a royal investigation was set up. It was then that Grey and his filthy friends were shown to be traitors! Death is too good for scum like this! . . .

FROGS ON THE HOP!
HARFLEUR IS TAKEN!!

Great King Harry! That's what they're calling him in France as he cuts his way through swarms of cowering Frogs. And it's ordinary, good-hearted, honest blokes like these who are helping him to do it. (From the left, Pistol, Bardolph and Nym.) Enjoy your celebration, lads! The Sun says you deserve every minute of it . . .

DEATH DRAMA FOR SUN'S HEROES!!!

The cheery faces of Bardolph and Nym, seen in yesterday's Sun, will laugh no more. A hero's death awaited them shortly after that heart-warming picture was taken. But the Sun has promised that their names will not be forgotten . . .

WHERE THE HELL'S HAL???
DISGUISE SCARE ON EVE OF BATTLE!!!

England's main strike force and the hero of Harfleur, Henry, the King himself, went missing last night! For some hours officials searched high and low for the much-loved monarch. Then the truth was revealed. The Royal Rogue had been visiting his men – in disguise!!

REJOICE!! REJOICE!!

England met France at Agincourt yesterday. The Sun is proud to report the result: England 10,999; France 29! And that's official! . . .

HERO HAL'S FRENCH DISH!!!

The man who crushed the enemies of Truth and Freedom at Agincourt conquered another Frog yesterday. This time he didn't need his sword or lance, though. The Frog in question is Princess Katharine, shapely daughter of the dispirited French King. Hal just swept her off her feet as easily as he would a troop of Froggie soldiers! Now we'll see whether the fairy tale is really true. Can a kiss from Handsome Harry turn a frog into a True Princess?

N.J.WARBURTON

WILLIAM SHAKESPEARE:
Julius Caesar

The chief defect of Julius C.,
One not unknown to you and me,
Was wanting to be Number One;
Thus spoiling all the Senate's fun.
He also liked men that were fat,
Proving he was no democrat.

There therefore was a nasty plot,
Whereby one Cassius and his lot
Decided to dispatch the ogre,
And let him have it, through the toga.

Oozing like a tutti-frutti,
Caesar murmured: *Et tu, Brute*.

One lesson from this ancient story –
Those who get immortal glory
Aren't too verbose and talkative:
They keep it short, and use the vocative.

When Julius C. had breathed his last,
A party political broadcast
Was made by Antony (three cheers),
Who told the plebs to lend their ears,
And into Cassius put the sandal.
The thing went off like a Roman candle,
So Brutus, Cassius & Co.
(When you gotta go, you gotta go),
Inexorably bound to lose
Because of Antony's '*J'accuse*',
Punctured and leaking like a sieve,
Expired, in the accusative.

W.S.BROWNLIE

WILLIAM SHAKESPEARE:
King Lear

GONERIL/REGAN: Pop's tops!
LEAR: True, Cordelia?
CORDELIA: Oh *Dad* –
LEAR: I banish you!
KENT: Gad!
LEAR: Vanish!
FOOL: Mad:
           Believe me, these sisters
           Deceive you.
LEAR: The twisters!
GLOUCESTER: And my boy's a bastard.
EDMUND: Too bad.
EDGAR: I'm disguised. Tom's a fruitcake.
LEAR: Me too.
GONERIL/REGAN: Prise those eyes out.
GLOUCESTER: I'm blinded! Boo-hoo!
EDMUND: I fix my own odds.
GLOUCESTER: The Gods are such sods.
EDGAR: No, they're not. Jump! All right?
GLOUCESTER: And that's true.
REGAN: My hubby's just snuffed it. To bed!
EDMUND: My lady?
GONERIL: He's mine!
ALBANY: You're still wed.
LEAR: The law is an ass;
           Forgive me, my lass.
CORDELIA: Of course!
REGAN: Ugh!
GONERIL: Agh!
EDMUND: Ooh!
ALBANY: They're all dead.
           Good old gods! Three cheers!
KENT: I feel queer.
LEAR: She's dead. Howl. Fool. Gurgle.
ALBANY: Oh dear.
KENT: He's dead, and I'm dying.
EDGAR: It's time to start crying.
ALBANY: I'm king. That's your lot. Shed a tear.

BILL GREENWELL

WILLIAM SHAKESPEARE:
Macbeth

MACDUFF Hold it! Are you, perchance, one Macbeth, self-styled
monarch of the glen, formerly Thane of Glamis and
Cawdor, what three witches put the evil eye on? Whose
baby-battering spouse helped you chop King Duncan and
blame his honest, law-abiding grooms, before she went
potty herself? The one what put the frighteners on the
royal princes, had your mate Banquo professionally
rubbished, my wife and chickens rubbed right out, can't
sleep, sees woods moving, has a complex about paternal
pregnancies, and waffles on and on and on about
tomorrow?

MACBETH Yes.

MACDUFF Right, lad, you're for the high jump.

BILL GREENWELL

WILLIAM SHAKESPEARE:
Macbeth

This is the life of Mac the Knife
     whose fate was foretold by witches:
They said he'd be King, so he and his wife
     worked out the possible hitches.
When good King Dunc in sleep was sunk,
     they thrust him through with a dagger,
And although poor Mac was blue with funk
     he carried it off with a swagger.
The King was dead, the princes fled,
     and the kingdom Mac's for the taking,
But Banq's for the chop since the witches said
     his sons were kings in the making.
The thugs are slow off the mark, and so
     they half-complete their mission,
But enough to make Mac's party go
     when he sees Banq's apparition;
This bloodstained ghost upsets the host
     but makes him even keener

To put his enemies on toast,
      and take them to the cleaner.
The witches bluff him with some stuff
      which is truthful yet deceiving;
His target is now the tough Macduff,
      who's off to England, leaving
His wife and chicks to cross the Styx,
      fit tidings to incite him
To end the tyrant's testy tricks,
      so he joins the prince to fight him.
Meanwhile the Knife observes his wife
      parade, out-out-damn-spotting –
Curses the shadow-play of life,
      such pointless parts allotting.
Now branches hood his foes – not good
      for Mac, who, white as linen,
Recalls what's said of Birnam Wood
      advancing to Dunsinane.
Still he won't run – no woman's son
      slays this predestinarian . . .
Macduff explains he isn't one
      (a posthumous Caesarian);
His sword goes smack through poor old Mac –
      alas for realm and riches!
It's better to endure their lack
      than put your trust in witches.

MARY HOLTBY

WILLIAM SHAKESPEARE:
The Merchant of Venice

Bassanio's a noble who needs lots of lolly
To woo his fair Portia, a very rich dolly.

He fingers his buddy, Antonio, for ducats,
So Tony then chats up a chap who has buckets:

Shylock the usurer, Merchant of Venice
(Who's locally reckoned a bit of a menace).

Shylock says: 'Okay, I'll lend you a stack
– For a pound of your flesh, if I don't get it back!'

Bassanio gets rich. A party game's played:
Bassanio wins Portia (his pal gets her maid).

Tony's fleet's wrecked; old Shylock now pounces,
And stakes out his claim for T.'s sixteen ounces.

Portia's the lawyer (she's dressed as a man);
Bassanio's fooled (believe that if you can!).

'No flesh without blood!' the Duke's Court decrees,
So Shylock is screwed by a neat legal wheeze.

They grab all his riches (but spare him his fate):
Half goes to Tony and half to the State.

'Convert!' says Antonio. 'And then all your bread
Will go to your daughter when you are dead!'

(Shylock's young daughter has married a goy,
Instead of the right kind of nice Jewish boy.)

Shylock's persuaded. All ends well, in short,
And T.'s battered boats come safely to port.

RON RUBIN

WILLIAM SHAKESPEARE:
The Merry Wives of Windsor

'Sir John in love' – his amorous rage
Embraces *Mesdames* Ford and Page;
Since twice his ample heart is troubled
So are his protestations doubled:
The duo find one billet-doux
Designed to do the work of two.
Such thrift deserves a rich reward,
Received when Falstaff visits Ford:

His bulk – convincingly to mask it –
Stuffed in a dirty linen basket,
Escapes the master's eye – to shiver,
Spread-eagled in a filthy river.
Though damped, such ardour cannot flag;
He makes a second try – in drag.
The master views the horrid sight
And in the beldame beats the knight.
Now wives and mates together plan
The downfall of this massive man.
In Windsor Forest's midnight shade
Shall love be lavishly displayed
And ladies drop their last defences
In a great banquet of the senses.
Meanwhile the Pages' daughter, Anne,
Has organised a private plan:
The groom her parents' hearts are bent on
She swaps for the attractive Fenton.
A sourer rendezvous for Jack,
Whom unseen sprites jab, nip and smack,
Till, cured at last of his sexperiment,
He joins the housewives in their merriment.

MARY HOLTBY

WILLIAM SHAKESPEARE:
A Midsummer Night's Dream

THESEUS [*Entering.*]
   Now to our nuptials all events are leading.
HIPPOLYTA [*Entering.*]
   Since I kept dogs I have been fond of breeding.
EGEUS [*Entering.*]
   Marry Demetrius!
HERMIA [*Entering.*]   Oh, no! Not him!
LYSANDER [*Entering.*]
   I'm her feller.
DEMETRIUS [*Entering.*]
               You are just a whim.

THESEUS

Obey thy father or become a nun;

Tomorrow morning shall his will be done.

[*Exeunt all but Lysander and Hermia.*]

LYSANDER

To the woods, my love. We'll no longer stay.

HELENA [*Entering.*]

But first tell me or there will be no play.

[*Exeunt omnes.*]

QUINCE [*Entering with rustics.*]

We'll do a play. Theseus likes the arts.

BOTTOM [*As they all exit.*]

I'll play Pyramus and all the parts.

OBERON [*Entering.*]

You're a bloody fairy!

TITANIA [*Entering.*]   And you're another!

No fancy boy for you. I knew his mother. [*Exit.*]

OBERON [*As Puck enters.*]

Oh. Puck! Give her one in the eye, and she'll feel randy.

PUCK

I find eye lotions very handy.

[*Exeunt omnes.*]

OBERON [*Entering.*]

My queen has kissed her Bottom!

PUCK [*Entering.*]   Elastic fairy!

I juiced up some Athenians all unwary.

[*Sounds of quarrelling off.*]

OBERON

You've buggered up their sex life, it meseems.

PUCK

They'll blame it all on their midsummer dreams.

DEMETRIUS [*Entering.*]

I love thee, Helena.

HELENA [*Entering.*]   I am so glad.

LYSANDER [*Entering.*]

I'm your feller now.

HERMIA [*Entering.*]   I'm really mad!

[*They sleep. Puck puts juice on their eyes.*]

TITANIA [*Entering.*]
  I've had such trouble with my great big ass.
OBERON [*As lovers awake.*]
  Scratch it, my love. The trouble will soon pass.
    [*Exeunt fairies.*]
LOVERS
  Now we know who is going to marry who.
THESEUS [*Entering with train.*]
  We'll hear a play.
HIPPOLYTA   And then we'll go and screw.
BOTTOM [*Entering as Pyramus.*]
  Here's Thisbe's scarf, and so I died. [*Dies.*]
FLUTE [*Enters as Thisbe.*]
  What dead, my love? Now me for suicide! [*Dies*]
THESEUS
  Enough, enough! There's no more to be said.
HIPPOLYTA
  At long last, now it is time for bed.
    [*Exeunt omnes.*]
PUCK [*Entering.*]
        Did no one call?
        No cry nor cough?
          Our play is o'er.
            So now – Puck off! [*Exit*]

                              E.O.PARROTT

WILLIAM SHAKESPEARE:
Much Ado about Nothing

Messina houses Beatrice, who's been known for wit and scorn
Since underneath a dancing star a dancing girl was born.
Messina is excited as it's never been before:
Pedro of Arragon is coming from the war.

Dim Dons jobbing while the Watch plays hell
(Beatrice and Benedick can argue rather well).
Hero is a heroine, Claudio a poop
(Don John of Arragon has put him in the soup).

         ... in One Evening

'Kill,' cries Beatrice. 'Claudio must pay!'
But Dogberry and Verges are the heroes of the day.
Their patter rocks the steeples, but it rings the wedding bells;
And Don John of Arragon is rotting in the cells.

PAUL GRIFFIN

WILLIAM SHAKESPEARE:
Othello

What the Papers Said

GIRL WITH EVERYTHING ASKS FOR MOOR

SOME OF MY BEST FRIENDS ARE CHILD-ABDUCTORS SENATOR CLAIMS

BLACK DAY FOR TURKS IN CYPRUS

DIRTY TRICKS IN ARMY PROMOTION SCANDAL

C.O.'S BRIDE IN SEX GAMES QUERY

WIFE SMOTHERED AFTER HANKIE HANKY-PANKY

HIT-MAN FLUFFS CYPRUS CONTRACT

MAN WITH BRIEFS IN DEAD WOMAN INNOCENT SHOCK

GENERAL DESPAIR IN EASTERN MEDITERRANEAN

SUICIDE SOLDIER IN MISUSE OF ARMY WEAPONS PROBE.

TIM HOPKINS

WILLIAM SHAKESPEARE:
Richard II

By banning two Dukes at a stroke
(One is Norfolk and one's Bolingbroke),
  King Richard the Second
  Has foolishly reckoned
His kingdom is now okey-doke.

And when time-honoured Lancaster fears
For this England, this plot without peers,
  This right royal throne,
  This so-precious stone,
King Richard at him only sneers.

But Bolingbroke comes back and takes
Richard's kingdom away, and he makes
  Him a pris'ner at Pontefract
  (You rhyme this with Humphrey),
Where Richard broods on his mistakes.

Now the time has arrived for a wallow
In self-pity – the crown is but hollow.
  He talks of sad things,
  Epitaphs, worms and kings,
And death, which is all that can follow.

So follow it does. To be brief,
He is murdered, and this ends his grief,
  As well as his days.
  It is one of the plays
Sadly lacking in comic relief.

JOYCE JOHNSON

WILLIAM SHAKESPEARE:
Richard III

In Richard the Third we behold a
Cold heart that could not have been colder;
    It is icy and black,
    For the crook on his back
Also gave him a chip on his shoulder.

So, with terrible villainy filled,
Due, he says, to his misshapen build,
    His scheming begins
    When he both woos and wins
The wife of the Edward he's killed.

He sends Clarence towards his last hour,
And the Princes are killed in the Tower,
    Hastings, Rivers and Grey
    Are dispatched the same way,
And we see the corruption of power.

Thanks to Buckingham, Richard is crowned.
Once firmly enthroned, though, it's found
    Good friends are forgotten
    And treated real rotten,
So Buckingham changes his ground.

But Nemesis comes in due course
When a kingdom is taken by force,
    And, finally snared,
    King Richard's prepared
To swap the whole thing for a horse.

JOYCE JOHNSON

WILLIAM SHAKESPEARE:
Romeo and Juliet

If you go down to the vault tonight, you're sure of a big surprise;
If you go down to the vault tonight, it mightn't be very wise;
      But if you dare, you'd better take care:
      There's Montague blood on the bill of fare –
Tonight's the night the Capulets have their picnic.

If you go down to the vault tonight, beware Mercutio's ghost;
He won't sit down in the vault tonight with an uncongenial host.
      Though unaware of his friend's affair –
      The secret troth – the dawn's despair –
The flight – he'll spite the Capulets at their picnic.

When you go down to the vault tonight to play at knuckle-bones,
He'll haunt his murderer's vault tonight (who hears his puns, and
   groans);
      It's Tybalt there, that swordsman rare –
      Got his when Romeo went off spare:
A sight to fright the Capulets at their picnic.

If you go down to the vault tonight, you'll see poor Paris too;
He just turned up at the vault tonight and Romeo ran him through;
      He's said a prayer for his Juliet where
      She lay in her bridal robes so fair –
Delightful sight for Capulets at their picnic.

When you go down to the vault tonight, you're sure to shiver and shake:
The Friar's gone down to the vault tonight, his dopey charge to wake;
      But she woke to stare at Romeo there,
      Who'd thought her dead and, mad to share
Her plight (quite right), joined Capulets at their picnic.

If you go down to the vault tonight on one of your graveyard trips,
You'll find a genuine corpse all right – poor Juliet's had her chips.
      A nasty scare greets the rivals there:
      For the starcrossed pair they'll all forswear
Their right to fight, from this frightsome night
When the Capulets had their picnic.

MARY HOLTBY

WILLIAM SHAKESPEARE:
The Taming of the Shrew

Caustic Kate insults her suitor;
'Courteous, gentle', he asserts her;
When he's got her, how he hurts her,
Like a veritable brute, a
Monster in his vile tormenting . . .
Biddable Bianca's cuter –
Fiddles in a 'music tutor',
Nuptials undesired preventing;
Swain, rebuffed, seeks consolation.

Happy husbands slyly stage a
Wives' Obedience Test, and wager
Who'll to marriage prove most fitted.
Contrary to expectation
Kate alone wins through; alerts her
Sisters to their wifely duty,
Pointing out the truer beauty
Found in those who have submitted.
Kate's commended, courted, kissed . . .

Shame on Shakespeare, chauvinist!

MARY HOLTBY

WILLIAM SHAKESPEARE:
The Tempest

Do you remember an Isle, Miranda?
     Do you remember an Isle?
And the sounds and sweet airs
That were Prospero's cares,
When the nearest man was Ca-Caliban,
     And Ariel offered the solaces?
Do you remember an Isle, Miranda?
     Do you remember an Isle?
Where Ariel's magic seemed suddenly tragic

When he led Ferdinand a
>   Dance round the policies
>   Teasing him many a mile;
Do you remember an Isle, Miranda?
>   Do you remember an Isle?

And the Ding-dang-dong,
And the song,
And the 'scapes and japes as the shapes
Went dancing, masquing,
Dinner-for-the-asking,
Putting all the plotters in a spin,
Out-and-in
Through a blizzard from the wizard for a while?
Do you remember an Isle, Miranda?
>   Do you remember an Isle?

Nevermore, Miranda, nevermore,
Only an unknown shore
And the chattering of courtiers at the door;
No bells or knells from the spells
Of your father, rather
The troubles of a queen, when you've been
Much more.

PAUL GRIFFIN

WILLIAM SHAKESPEARE:
Timon of Athens

LORD TIMON
*Who, on Finding that his Flatterers were False Friends,
Became Much Embittered*

Lord Timon, an example he
Of over-liberality,
Lavished his gifts on one and all.
His home indeed was Welcome Hall.
If any guest admired a thing,
A jewel, say, or priceless Ming,
Timon would say: 'My friend, please take it.'

If touched for any sum, he'd make it
Twice as much. He did them proud.
And thus it was he drew a crowd
Of smooth-tongued toadies, not real friends,
Who flattered him to gain their ends.

Until at last there came the day
He had more bills than he could pay.
But not to worry – he had lots
Of friends who owed him simply pots,
And he was sure that some of them
Would gladly help him out *pro tem* .
But did they pay up? They did not.
Was ever such an ingrate lot?

Timon then hit upon a plan.
He asked each so-called gentleman
To grace once more his loaded table.
These trencher-friends who'd been unable
To pay these debts that had been owing,
Hearing of something better going,
Came trooping in, of course, like mad:
'Good sir, we were so very sad
We could not help you yesterday.'
Timon replied: 'Be seated, pray.'
This done, he next addressed them thus:
'I see that you are ravenous,
Let each one fill his hungry gap –
Uncover, dogs,' he cried, 'and lap!'

The guests complied, as they were bid,
And each one lifted up a lid.
What lay beneath? They peered, and lo!
Nothing was there but H_2O!
And then, to make bad matters worse,
Timon abused them with a curse,
Flinging the water in their faces –
No wonder that they fled their places!
'A host who gives us only water –
Really,' they said, 'he didn't oughter!'

It's time to cut this story short.
So, having been so rudely taught
That servile praise and bended knee
Were naught but cupboard love, Lord T.
Of human nature gave up hope,
And lived and died a Misanthrope.

  Moral
Lend money, friends, if lend you must,
Only to people you can trust.

  JOYCE JOHNSON

WILLIAM SHAKESPEARE:
Twelfth Night

Once upon a time was a useful little wreck –
  With a heigh-ho, the wind and the rain –
When twins were washed right off the deck
  And each thought the other was lifeless clay.

The girl, dressed male, served a lovelorn lord –
  With a heigh-ho, the grief and the pain –
But herself the gloomy duke adored,
  While she wooed the lady who said him nay.

The lady's uncle, her maid and clown –
  With a heigh-ho, a knight *sans* brain –
By her pompous steward were so put down,
  That they planned together to make him pay.

They forged a letter of love professed –
  With a heigh-ho, the bird is ta'en –
He dressed like a guy at the lady's hest,
  And leered till she had him put away.

Meanwhile Twin Two appears in the town –
  With a heigh-ho, (what a trite refrain!) –
Meets the lady, the knight, the uncle, the clown,
  And wonders whether his wit's astray.

For the lady, who'd taken a shine to his twin,
    With a heigh-ho, has a groom to gain;
And the mess the look-alikes find themselves in
    Involves affiance, offence, affray.

When all's revealed and peace restored –
    With a heigh-ho – it's a bit of a strain –
One twin weds lady, the other lord,
    And that (more or less) is the end of the play.

MARY HOLTBY

WILLIAM SHAKESPEARE:
The Winter's Tale

[*Enter Polixenes, Leontes and Hermione.*]

LEONTES 'Ere! Wot's your game?

HERMIONE Eh?

LEONTES You 'eard. Wotcher up to wiv 'im?

HERMIONE 'Oo?

LEONTES Polixenes.

POLIXENES She in't up to nuffin wiv me.

LEONTES Oh yeah?

POLIXENES Chance'd be a fine thing.

LEONTES Wossat s'posed to mean?

[*Enter Paulina.*]

PAULINA You wanna watch yerself, you do.

LEONTES Shut yer face!

HERMIONE Now what?

LEONTES And you! Tart! Go on, piss off, the pair of you!

[*Exeunt Hermione, Polixenes and Paulina.*]

LEONTES I'll do fer 'im, you see if I don't. [*Exit.*]

[*Enter Leontes and Antigonus.*]

LEONTES I've 'ad enough of this! Muckin' me about!

ANTIGONUS Wot?

LEONTES You c'n jest git shot of that slut. And the kid!

[*Exit Antigonus. Enter Cleomenes and Dion.*]

CLEOMENES Oi!

LEONTES Wot?

DION She in't done nuffin.

LEONTES Wot?

CLEOMENES You 'eard. We jest paged the Oracle.

LEONTES Oh Gawd!
[*Exeunt. Enter Antigonus and Mariner.*]

ANTIGONUS Where the 'ell are we?

MARINER Bo'emia. [*Exit Mariner.*]

ANTIGONUS The baby's bleedin' 'eavy. Crikey! 'Sa bear! I'm orf!
[*Exit. Enter a Shepherd and Autolycus.*]

SHEPHERD Blimey! A kid!

AUTOLYCUS Lend us a quid.

SHEPHERD Shove off!

AUTOLYCUS Gi's a job.

SHEPHERD You 'eard. [*Exeunt.*]
[*Later. Enter Florizel and Perdita.*]

FLORIZEL Cor!

PERDITA Wossat s'posed ter mean?

FLORIZEL Wotcher think, gal?

PERDITA Yeah. Well, I might. Oo are yer, anyway?
[*Enter Polixenes, disguised.*]

POLIXENES Oi! Cut that out!

FLORIZEL You mind yours, sunshine!

POLIXENES Oh yeah? [*Discovering himself.*]

FLORIZEL Crikey! Let's git out of 'ere, gal!
[*Exeunt. Enter Leontes.*]

LEONTES I'm bored.
[*Enter Perdita, Florizel and Polixenes.*]

PERDITA Dad!

LEONTES Blimey! What a turn-up!

POLIXENES You 'er old man, then?

LEONTES Yeah.
[*Enter Paulina.*]

PAULINA I told yer, din't I? You made a right pig's ear o' this!

LEONTES S'pose so.
[*Paulina brings on Hermione as a statue.*]

LEONTES Wot the 'ell's that, then?

PAULINA Wotsit look like?

LEONTES Statue?

HERMIONE Yeah. 'S me, all right.

LEONTES Stone me!

N. J. WARBURTON

GEORGE BERNARD SHAW:
Androcles and the Lion

In Africa a Christian tailor, Androcles by name,
Removed a thorn from out a lion's paw.
The grateful beast decided that it ought to play the game
And waive, for once, the law of tooth and claw.

Years later, at Rome's Coliseum, Christian prisoners stood,
Awaiting leonine extermination.
The Christian girl, Lavinia, displayed much fortitude
In dealing with this trying situation.

The Captain of the Guard explained she could be free again,
Provided . . . hereupon he popped the question.
She told him Christian women *never* marry heathen men,
But thanked him for his civilised suggestion.

A friend of hers, Ferrovius – a mighty man was he –
Within the ring slew several gladiators.
The Emperor, extremely pleased, set all the prisoners free,
Which much annoyed the stadium spectators.

To soothe them, just one Christian would become a lion's
    snack –
The choice of Androcles was automatic.
The lion picked (you've guessed it?) he remembered from
    way back . . .
Their long-delayed reunion was ecstatic!

The Captain and Lavinia? She did not change her mind.
(Christians could never *marry* heathen men!)
But since a Christian maiden has a duty to be kind,
He could come round and see her now and then.

                                        T.L.McCARTHY

GEORGE BERNARD SHAW:
Pygmalion

27A Wimpole Street,
London, W.1.
19.11.1911

A. B. Carruthers, Esq., D.E.F.,
The Reader, Department of Phonetics,
University of Oxford.

Dear Carruthers,

Regarding my appearance at your language symposium next week, I am afraid my lecture will be not quite as promised. The young Cockney female who was taught to speak like a duchess, and was supposed to accompany me on the platform for demonstration purposes, has, for some inexplicable reason, deserted my household (she was a live-in pupil), and I will be obliged to make do with the phonograph machine and wax cylinders. Her desertion represents a rather sad ending to an interesting experiment. She has attained a unique place in the history of phonetics by adding three wholly new vowel sounds and a number of hybrids to the Audio Index. You will doubtless agree with me that she has, accordingly, little to complain about.

You will recall Colonel Pickering's famous claret 'tastings' where the guests were blindfolded and asked to determine vintages – remember the spree with the Algerian Ordinary? I held a phonetics 'hearing' the other evening along similar lines and it was a great success. The winner was Miss Clara Eynsford-Hill, who has a remarkable ear. She would have scored full marks but for one error when she mistook the recorded screams of Miss Doolittle (the young Cockney female) on introduction to her first bath for the sound of a tom-cat being neutered without benefit of chloroform. It was a splendid effort none the less.

Pickering thinks that Eliza (the young Cockney female) might well return, and I am almost certain he is right. My housekeeper, Mrs Pearce, however, rather doubts this and contends that there was an air of finality in the hand signal Eliza transmitted to me just before leaving, which has apparently some arcane significance among the working classes. I have always understood this finger display to indicate 'It takes two to make a quarrel', but Mrs Pearce has hinted that I may be wrong. Could you have a word with Dalrymple of Anthropology next time you see him?

There is some talk of Eliza marrying Freddy (Clara's fool of a brother) and opening a flower shop. If she does she will need a further course of lessons. Although she can pass herself off as a duchess now, talking like a lady in a flower shop (as she phrases it) is an entirely different matter.

See you at the symposium

Yours sincerely,

Henry Higgins

T.L.McCARTHY

GEORGE BERNARD SHAW:
Saint Joan

A field somewhere in Normandy. Two people confront one another on a path in the middle of the field.

GOD: Joan of Arc, I presume . . .

JOAN [*excited*]: My God . . . it's You. I recognise the voice.

GOD: You have an excellent ear. Have you ever considered studying phonetics?

JOAN: I'm hell-bent on being a saint. Once I've raised the siege of Orleans and crowned the Bastard at Rheims, my career will be significantly advanced . . .

GOD: You're forgetting . . . capture by the English, the Inquisition, torture, humiliation and the stake . . .

JOAN [*happily*]: And after that . . . canonisation . . .

GOD: One shouldn't aspire to sainthood in quite the same way as one aspires to be an accountant or a pork-pie manufacturer.

JOAN: I will acquire great spiritual merit by squashing the loathsome English.

GOD: Commitment to political violence might transform you into a national heroine, Joan, but sainthood is altogether a more elevated business.

JOAN: What about my voices? St Catherine . . . St Margaret . . .
You . . . Oh, how i adore that soft lilting sound of Yours.

GOD: It's just a common or garden, middle-class Dublin accent, my
       child. [*Solemnly*] Now you must never disclose to the
       English that God is a middle-class Irishman. They will
       almost certainly believe you and ... poof! goes your chance
       of glorious martyrdom and sainthood.
JOAN: I can't wait to join You in Heaven ...
GOD: We're in Hertfordshire at present ...
JOAN: I love You.
GOD: And don't get any amorous ideas. Being the embodiment of
       sex, I'd frizzle you up the moment you approached Me
       with even a hint of impure intent.
JOAN: Ah ... I shall remember that when I'm consumed by Your
       passion at the stake ...
GOD [*outraged*]: You're compromising Me, you little hussy. I shall
       punish you by making an exhibition of you on the English
       stage. I'll transform you into a dramatic character ...
JOAN [*horrified*]: You wouldn't dare ...

CURTAIN

RUSSELL LUCAS

MARY W. SHELLEY:
Frankenstein

The youthful Victor Frankenstein conceived a fabulous design
To make an artificial humanoid.
He'd studied chemistry at school and wasn't anybody's fool,
And thought he knew the pitfalls to avoid.

He tried a few dissections and some charnel-house inspections planned;
Then made a monster on a massive scale.
Although the frame was fine and strong, the eyes and lips went
    badly wrong.
The thing was more than eight feet tall – and male ...

At once appalled at what he'd done, young Frankenstein went on
    the run.
The monster, raging, set off in pursuit.
He strangled Victor's brother, then began pursuing *him* again;
On Mont Blanc, Victor faced up to the brute.

The creature, being celibate, expressed a wish to have a mate.
Vic started off repairing this omission.
But visions of a breeding pair, and little monsters everywhere,
Obliged him to abandon the commission.

The thing, incensed, then put an end to Clerval, Victor's lifelong
  friend;
Our hero vowed revenge with deep emotion.
The boot was on the other foot, now *Victor* set off in pursuit –
The monster headed towards the Arctic Ocean.

The drama heightened when a craft plucked Victor from an icy raft,
Weak and exhausted from his fruitless chase.
Later the creature was espied, intent, it seemed, on suicide;
It vanished in the darkness without trace.

Before he died aboard the ship, Vic left this very useful tip
For those who wish to fabricate Mammalia:
'Had I my time to live once more, I'd make my monster four feet four,
And wouldn't bother with the genitalia.'

T.L.McCARTHY

RICHARD BRINSLEY SHERIDAN:
The Rivals

Mrs Malaprop sums it up:

Captain Absolute is deeply enamelled of my niece, Lydia
Languish, a young lady with a very specious place in my inflections.
The Captain assumes the guiles of an Ensign, as my Lydia has refuted
the intentions of a baronet's heir, sperming his advances in favour of
a poorly ruminated young officer. Lydia receives the court of the
would-be soldier with the facetious commission, but she knows she
must lose percussion of half her fortune if she marries without my
consort. And I will not acquiesce in bequests for intercourse with a
subaltern.

Sir Anthony arrives at Bath, but he is not continent with
the facts discerning his son. He therefore prepuces a match between
Lydia and Captain Absolute: this I have every intention of bringing
to a satisfying contusion, but the Captain is afraid of reviling his

cunning centrifuge to Lydia. He has a rival, too, in Bob Acres, who asks Absolute to send a challenge to the factitious ensign at the installation of Sir Lucius O'Trigger, an open-mouthed flame-masturbator. Sir Lucius challenges Captain Absolute, having mistaken my handwritten letters as apostles from my niece. But when Acres discovers that the Ensign is his friend Absolute, he naturally reclines to fight. Sir Lucius is self-abused by my arrival, and Lydia, after a spirited, but brief, alteration with her lover, finally forgoes him.

TIM HOPKINS

ALAN SILLITOE:
The Loneliness of the Long Distance Runner

Borstal boy,
Splendid jogger,
Runs for joy.
Stubborn bogger

Throws a race
Just to see
Governer's face,
Thinks: 'Tee-Hee!'

Written shorter
(Saving ink):
'Horse at water
Need not drink.'

V. ERNEST COX

ALAN SILLITOE:
Saturday Night and Sunday Morning

In the scrag end of Nottingham City,
As is noted for supping and sin,
Arthur Seaton, a canny machinist,
Would loosen up lasses with gin;

If they'd husbands – well, that was their problem,
So Brenda, Jack's missus, was first:
Arthur charmed her, his chat was like bubbles –
Transparent and ready to burst.

But he didn't take much to the notion,
Of curbing what preachers call lust,
So he wasn't surprised when two squaddies,
Left him covered in blood, sweat and dust.

At work he found little excitement,
So he dreamt of his passionate nights,
All grist to the mill of his fancy,
The mem'ry of Brenda's delights.

Now Brenda had heard of heartbreakers,
Who are selfish, capricious and wild,
But none the less offered him favours,
Well, at least, till she carried his child.

Then straightway the brave little woman,
Without showing panic or fear,
Drank gin in a bathtub of water,
While Arthur had chasers of beer.

Now Winnie was Brenda's young sister,
Not pregnant, and sweetly endowed.
Arthur's eyes were alert to her body,
A body of which she was proud;

They loved, but the truth was discovered,
So hubby, a good-natured chap,
Drove his old Morris car straight at Arthur,
Which Arthur turned over as scrap.

Next was Doreen, a comely young maiden,
At nineteen untutored in life,
Who pouted when Arthur got frisky:
'How dare you, we're not man and wife!'

Their discussions of love and of marriage
Force Arthur to make a U-turn,
Controlling the promptings of Satan,
Denying the passions which burn.

If there's moral at all in this story,
Then nice girls must never forget:
When it comes to securing an Arthur,
If you give all you've got, you won't get.

TIM HOPKINS

C. P. SNOW:
The Affair

'Are you awake, Sometime Fellow in Palaeontology?' The
speaker sounded wrought-up, possessed, slightly agitated.

His interlocutor awoke with a snort. He looked
considerably older than his ninety-seven years, his skin as scraggy
and flaccid as that of an ill-conditioned vulture; though the academic
gown that mouldered gently on his shoulders – and that he was
reputed never to have doffed since the outbreak of the First War –
put one more in mind of a peculiarly decrepit pterodactyl.

'What is it, what is it?' he hissed with dyspeptic testiness
that it had taken seventy years of Founder's Port to mature.

'You remember Howard?'

'Howard? Howard? There have been so many Howards.'

'Admittedly. It is a name once noble but now, alas,
lamentably banal. Even the working classes use it, I am told, to label
their male offspring. Anyway, the Howard I mean is the one we kicked
out of the college.'

'Which college?'

'This college. Our college.'

'I'll take your word for it, Manciple Emeritus Honorificus.
What did we kick him our for?'

'Faking part of his research.'

'How?'

'He forged a diffraction photograph.'

'The devil he did.'

'He blew it up.'

'Blew who up?'

Really, it was about time the old boy had his ear-trumpet rebored again on the National Health. 'Anyway, it now seems he may not have done it after all.'

'Who did then?'

'It seems it could have been Palairet, his professor.'

'Palairet? But he's even more senile than I am – impossible though that may be to believe.'

'Senility may have been the reason for his doing it.'

'I certainly find it a wonderful excuse for shoplifting.'

'Anyway, the old boy's dead.'

'With Palairet, that was not the sort of thing one would ever have noticed.'

'There may have been another reason for his doing it.'

'What?'

'Vanity.'

'Ah – that vice most incident to academics. The only true begetter of a million unwanted monographs.'

'On the other hand, after Palairet's death Nightingale may have tampered with his papers in a fashion calculated to incriminate Howard.'

'Why?'

'He hated him.'

'My dear fellow, all dons hate one another. That's the basic axiom of academic life – and its only really enduring pleasure.'

'At all events, proof now seems so impossible of procurement that the Court of Seniors have decided to reinstate him.'

'Who?'

'Howard.'

'Howard?'

'Oh my God – haven't you been listening?'

'Not listening to what other people say is the only way in which the old can retain their sanity.'

'Anyway, the matter's now closed.'

'And do you mean to tell me that you woke me up just to recite this unutterably tedious little story?'

'Well, Lewis Elliot is writing a whole book about it.'

'He *would*. Do you know what it is, of *all* the many insufferable things about that fellow, that I find the most unendurable of all?'

'What?'

'The way he tries to have it all ways. He's more incorrigibly
Establishment-minded than anyone else I've ever met, yet at the same
time he's always referring to himself as "an odd man out", as one of
"those outside, pushing their noses against the shop-window". Sheer
self-deception. And in all his wretched, stilted, self-applauding
fictions, he makes us out to be the most small-minded bunch of
malicious, intriguing pettifoggers you could ever conceive – and then
expects us to be grateful for the portrait! He's – but why, pray, are
you pulling those awful faces at me? Oh, Lewis – didn't hear you
come in – we were just singing your praises, dear boy ...'

MARTIN FAGG

ALEXANDER SOLZHENITSYN:
Cancer Ward

'O what ails thee, Kostoglotov,
Alone on Ward 8 landing,
The colour drained from both thy cheeks,
And no Kurds sing?

'O what ails thee, Kostoglotov,
So withered and so scant of hair,
When X-ray lists are teeming full,
And committees care?

'I see disturbance on thy brow,
With sweating face and stomach pained,
And in thine eyes a fading hope;
Thy lips are pale and strained.

'A party member on the ward,
Denounced you an awkward sort,
Complaining thou didst speak too soon,
That exiles count for naught.

'I made a plea on thy behalf,
And others, too, stressed thy good stock;
They looked at me as they did smile,
And made sweet mock.

'And thy young Zoya, did she offer love,
A kiss in the nurses' room?
For always now she laughs and sings,
Farewell to gloom.

'And solemn Gangart, did she care?
I've seen her weep and sigh full sore;
One day I told her, love is pain;
I think she swore.

'But I've seen injections changing men,
Pale wraiths unsexed by drugs,
Who've cried: "Our manhood's taken!"
To cold, official shrugs.

'So this is why you sojourn here,
Alone on Ward 8 landing,
The colour drained from both thy cheeks,
And no Kurds sing.'

TIM HOPKINS

JOHN STEINBECK:
The Grapes of Wrath

Across the country trek the migrant Joads,
Impoverished, uprooted, dispossessed,
With other Okies thronging dusty roads
That disappear towards the Golden West.
Society and nature do their worst.
Impediments galore beset their trail.
The Land of Opportunity seems cursed:
The greedy flourish and the honest fail.
And when at last the family arrives
In California's orchards, what they face

Are arduous, underpaid, peach-pickers' lives –
Short, nasty, brutish, squalid, poor and base.
O pity then the wretched of the earth:
Man eats and sleeps and fornicates and dies.
But wait! *The Grapes of Wrath* ends with a birth –
Negation does not win the Nobel Prize.

BASIL RANSOME-DAVIES

JOHN STEINBECK:
Of Mice and Men

Two working men named George and Lennie,
Who slaved away for every penny,
Dreamed, when their working days were over,
Of living, as it were, in clover
On their own spread in rural ease
With rabbits hopping round the trees.
But Lennie, though at heart a child,
Would, in a panic, grow so wild
That George, his minder, always feared
That Lennie would do something weird.
Alas! It happened. George's pal,
Teased by a wanton *femme fatale*,
The boss's son's seductive wife,
Freaked out and took the lady's life.
At which George, with an anguished frown
And smoking gun, put Lennie down.
The moral is that violent habits
Do not consort with keeping rabbits.

BASIL RANSOME-DAVIS

ROBERT LOUIS STEVENSON:
Treasure Island

Now somewhere down on the Plymouth line
Is 'The Admiral Benbow', with a creaking sign,
Where an old buccaneer decides to come
With a yo-ho-ho! and a bottle of rum.
> Listen, listen, all you young,
> Long John Silver has a golden tongue;
> He looks for the treasure in a dead man's chest –
> Now who do you think deserves it best?

In a tropical sea, in an island hid
Is a treasure that belonged to Captain Kidd,
And this buccaneer, who's a thirsty chap,
Has its whereabouts shown upon a map.
> Listen, listen, *etc.*

When drink and the devil have done for him,
The map goes to Mrs Hawkins's Jim;
He's only safe from the pirates when
Blind Pew's ridden down by the excisemen.
> Listen, listen, *etc.*

Jim tells the Squire, and they sail to sea,
With a crew on the verge of mutiny;
But when they're anchored in the waters blue,
Young Jim Hawkins knows a thing or two.
> Listen, listen, *etc.*

They find Ben Gunn in the island trees;
He's a long white beard, and he wants some cheese;
His wits have gone, for he's been there years,
But he helps them beat the mutineers.
> Listen, listen, *etc.*

This makes him a traitor to the working class,
For they find the treasure chest, bound in brass,
And the fruits of the workers' industry
Are handed over to the bourgeoisie.
> Listen, listen, *etc.*

PAUL GRIFFIN

ROBERT LOUIS STEVENSON:
Treasure Island

Six feet down lies a dead man's chest –
    Yo-ho-ho, and a treasure to come!
Black Dog, Black Spot and a black-souled guest,
    Scarred and scared and afloat with rum . . .

Charts and coins in a dead man's chest –
    Yo-ho-ho, and a treasure to come!
And off on a voyage to find the rest;
    The crew is crafty, the captain glum.

Doctor and squire and boy possessed
    (Yo-ho-ho!) with the treasure to come!
And a one-legged cook to foul the nest;
    The plot grows ripe, the three keep mum.

Battle and booze – and the baddies blessed
    (Yo-ho-ho!) with the treasure to come?
But the hole gapes wide and the loot's gone west,
    For mad Ben Gunn's pulled out the plum.

And dauntless Jim (a little pest) –
    Yo-ho-ho for the treasure to come! –
Spies, shoots and slashes with tiresome zest
    That leaves his foes and readers numb.

But all, of course, turns out for the best –
    Yo-ho-ho, and to boot, yum-yum!
The rum-soaked scum have queered their quest
    And home with the treasure the heroes come.

MARY HOLTBY

BRAM STOKER:
Dracula

I went to bed and read this horror book
(The hero's hair had turned white overnight!);
Count Dracula of Transylvania took
Flights overnight in search of necks to bite.
He was a vampire – one can always tell –
They cast no shadow and are rather scared
Of rosaries, and garlic plants as well . . .
(On Transylvanian coach tours – be prepared!)

The Count conceived a notion to acquire
An English landed property, and so
He sent for lawyer Harker to inquire
If he could recommend a place to go.
Harker survived some diabolic tricks
Before he managed to get back to Britain,
By the nice conduct of a crucifix,
He reached home with his jugular unbitten.

For vampires carry this type of infection –
In places where blood-sucking is endemic,
The victims have a vampire resurrection –
In no time, there's a bloody epidemic!
By methods which we need not detail here,
The Count could travel anywhere he chose.
The marks of neck-bites started to appear
On British citizens – after repose.

No one but Harker guessed the reason why!
He knew the remedy and journeyed back
To Transylvania. The Count must die!
He slit his throat in a surprise attack.
It's all described minutely in the book
(No wonder lawyer Harker's hair turned white!) –
Next morning when I went and had a look,
I found my . . . yes, you're absolutely right!

T.L.McCARTHY

DEAN JONATHAN SWIFT:
Gulliver's Travels

Letters from Gulliver

Lilliput

Arrival at beach a knock-out. Initially tied up, with locals all over me.
I'm very big here, but still have to watch my step. Height of shoe-
heels and methods of egg-cracking dominate conversation. They're
even prepared to go to war over such trifles. Would they had our
political maturity.

Lemuel

Brobdingnag

I look up to the natives – it's the only way. A farmer's daughter has
taught me the lingo, and she's now got me in the palm of her hand. A
new career as entertainer has opened up for me with people paying
big money to watch me. Their views on history are rather quaint.
According to them only the very worst people attain positions of
power. I mentioned Attila and Ghengis Khan by way of defence, but
their replies were unprintable.

Takes all sorts,

L.

Laputa

Air holiday! You're not jesting! Island in mid-air and approached
from underneath by pulley. Heads of locals incline to left or right.
Strange eyes, too: one regards the zenith, the other looks inwards.
(Hamlet could have used one of those!) Servants do all practical work
while men speculate fruitlessly on eccentric schemes. (Leaving others
to pleasure their wives.) Latest lines of inquiry are extracting
sunbeams from cucumber and turning excrement into food. (Food to
excrement they can do already!) Politics they adore, but they lack the
power to reason coherently (like the Pump Room at Bath, perhaps!).

Yours in good humour,

Lem

Magic! The Governor resurrects the illustrious dead for my amusement. Trouble is, Caesar and Alexander are quite unimpressive in the flesh. My host takes the view that all such leaders are cowardly, flattering and degenerate. Decent people, he asserts, never attain power. I told the Governor what he could do with his resurrections. What a relief our leaders back home are beyond reproach.

Your fortified,

Lemuel G.

Luggnagg

Having to crawl on my belly and lick the dust not to my taste, but 'When in Luggnagg . . .' as they say. And people never die here so I suppose everyone has the chance to get used to it. Immortality does have problems, though. Would you like to live eternally without hair, teeth, memory and speech? That's the fate of everyone here when they reach what we call senility. They are also cut off from contact with the world of the young and middle-aged. Not a lot of laughs here.

Your mortal,

L. Gulliver

The Houyhnhnms

These horse-like creatures with high levels of reasoning and spirituality share their land with the Yahoos, a disgusting group of four-legged hairy creatures with long nails. Curiously, they are somewhat human in appearance, although their constant fighting, theft and fornication is definitely not so. The Yahoos are also incapable of learning from past mistakes, again a characteristic rarely observed in humans. Yesterday my life here suffered an ignominious setback, when my master suggested I was inferior to the Yahoos owing to my short nails and single pair of legs. In spite of the Houyhnhnms' wisdom, compassion and generosity, I feel I must leave their country. The thought of living among humans again is repellent.

Glad you're not here,

Lemuel Gulliver

TIM HOPKINS

J. M. SYNGE:
The Playboy of the Western World

PATRICK, *shop assistant*
MICHAEL, *the local publican*

> *The conversation takes place in the general store of a Mayo village after the action of the play has been completed.*

MICHAEL [*entering*]: God save all here!

PATRICK: God save you kindly!

MICHAEL: Ah, it's glad enough I am to be out of the rain, out of God's leaking firmament, into the tidy wee shopland of a decent man ...

PATRICK: Can I be of assistance?

MICHAEL: Sure, 'tis destroyed I am. Did you see a gallous fiery young fellow and his old Da leaving the village, shouting and squabbling with raised tempers and great rages, calling down the blessed stars to witness ...

PATRICK: Yes, last night.

MICHAEL: ... and leaving me without a pot-boy at all, and the daughter of mine, Pegeen Mike, with her heart split down the middle worse than any female woman from here to Castlebar and herself wailing for the runaway pot-boy, the Playboy of the Western World, like a banshee screaming warnings of approaching death through the night's black draperies ...

PATRICK: That would be young Christie Mahon, who split his Da's head open? Sure, we thought he was a murderer and the girls went crazy for him. Both your Pegeen and the Widow Quin wanted to marry him, by all accounts.

MICHAEL: Until his Da turned up alive and kicking, more or less in one piece, with a hole in his napper you could have put your own head in, to be sure, like a hound dog searching the middens of Hell ...

PATRICK: It made a nonsense of the whole thing really. What can I get you?

MICHAEL: Sure, I've no food taken since Father Reilly's black cock announced the long dawn saving a supeen of porter and my stomach's thinking my throat's cut, so it is. I'll be after troubling you for a piece of the pride of Mayo, cut bravely in a middling hunk, thick at one end and sloping to a

thin edge at the other, the daily rental of a dacent herd,
and shining gold like the sunset over Crossmolina with
the bloom on it that would make the royal Pope and all his
Holy Cardinals ...

PATRICK: I'm sorry? I been over in Liverpool this last twelve months
and I seem to have lost the lilt.

MICHAEL: I'll have a pound of Irish Cheddar, please.

CURTAIN

T.L.McCARTHY

DYLAN THOMAS:
Under Milk Wood

1ST VOICE: *Down Your Way* this week visits the quaint little seaside
village of Llareggub in Wales with its quaint collection of
fishing boats bobbing in the harbour, its three quaint but
crowded streets and its quaintly bustling commercial
centre near 'The Sailor's Arms'. And I'm talking first of
all to the chap who keeps an eye on all the goings-on in
Llareggub. I understand you've been up and about very
early this morning.

2ND VOICE: Sleepless and silent I make my poem-crafting way to
window ledges ...

1ST VOICE: A poet? That sounds interesting.

2ND VOICE: Fag-dangling, rubber-lipped word-mouther and
monger, I tongue-trip through the mild beer froth ...

1ST VOICE: Really? How fascinating!

2ND VOICE: ... elbowing the sloped bar and pouring my rich, dark,
tree-coal black, treacle-black vowel-intoning voice into
the barmaid's pink, unlistening ear ...

1ST VOICE: Fancy that. [*Aside*] Jacky, can you do anything about
this? They aren't going to make head or tail of it in
Dorking.

JACKY TAPE-RECORDER: I did try to warn you, love.

2ND VOICE: ... prying from the distant-barking, bed-soft harking
shadows, I watch the nodding, dream and nightmare
calling flesh of Llareggub as it fingers through the sleep
and ...

1ST VOICE: Ha ha! Well, well. [*Aside*] Look, buy him another drink, Jacky, and then fade in 'Men of Harlech' or something. We can't go on like this.
[*Fade up 'Men of Harlech'.*]

1ST VOICE: We come now to . . .

2ND VOICE: Blind Captain Cat, seeing once more with his mind . . .

1ST VOICE: Oh no. Not again . . .

2ND VOICE: Rosie Probert, 33 Duck Lane, whom he shared with Tom-Fred the donkeyman . . .

1ST VOICE: Good grief!

2ND VOICE: . . . Polly Garter, stepping voluptuously through the milk-demanding muddle of her babies, approaching the yearning, soon-to-be-rewarded manhood of Llareggub as she plumps the pillow of her soft, white . . .

1ST VOICE: For goodness' sake, Jacky, get rid of him!
[*Sound of scuffling.*]

1ST VOICE: I am joined now by one Mr Willy Nilly, Llareggub's postman . . .

2ND VOICE: . . . steaming open frank and steamy letters and, for Mr Pugh, schoolmaster, poisonous plans to dispatch sour Mrs Pugh . . .

1ST VOICE: Stop him, Jacky! Quick!
[*Sound of a smashing bottle.*]

1ST VOICE: Well now, Mr Nilly. You must know Llareggub pretty . . . Aargh!

2ND VOICE [*groggily*]: . . . while Mae Rose Cottage, circling her nipples in lipstick . . .

1ST VOICE: Please, sir! People in Broadstairs will be listening to this!

2ND VOICE: . . . lush, life-delighting Cherry Owen staggers singing home as, sinning lewdly among the coarse bushes, Nogood Boyo and Lily Smalls . . .

1ST VOICE: Oh, this is hopeless. Let's scrub the whole thing and move on, Jacky. Things are bound to be better in Eastbourne.

N.J. WARBURTON

DYLAN THOMAS:
Under Milk Wood

O little town of Llareggub,
How still we see thee lie,
Then gradually the place wakes up
And, as the day goes by,
We hear the locals gossiping,
They prattle till nightfall,
Then off they go to bed again.
What's happened? – Bugger all.

V. ERNEST COX

J. R. R. TOLKIEN:
The Lord of the Rings

Whatever became of young Frodo?
A furry-toed, game little beast.
Is it true that he went off to Mordor, a no-go
Area in the Far East?
Remember that Sam,
The son of old Ham,
Who kept Bilbo's garden so trim?
Those two were quite thick, you know, like horse and groom,
And travelled together, but fell into gloom,
Until Frodo gave up, on the top of Mount Doom.
I wonder what happened to him!

Whatever became of old Strider?
He went about in disguise, doing good,
Constantly chased by a sinister Rider,
Who wore a black cloak and a hood.
You know, he got himself
Engaged to this Elf,
Though he was always so weathered and grim.
And after some mishaps by tunnel and crag,
Rushed off to Gondor, waving a flag;
They acclaimed him as king after nine centuries' lag.
I wonder what happened to him!

Whatever became of old Gandalf?
Him with the beard of waist-length.
Some Balrog in Khazad gave him a hand-off,
Down a chasm, but he got back his strength.
His staff would shoot sparks,
He made darkling remarks,
Which confounded his friends to the brim.
And he galloped about with a grey cloak and horse,
And his mystery backers had him winning, of course,
Which just goes to prove the success of Good Force.
I wonder what happened to him!

Whatever became of old Sauron?
With the evil, red, all-seeing eye,
Though he conducted his wars like a moron,
And couldn't catch a small Hobbit spy.
He always would hire
Orcs, whose desire
Was to slaughter each other with vim.
And, do you know, he invested his power
Into one single ring, so in one single hour,
It was melted, and crash! down came his Tower.
I wonder what happened to him!

REM BEL

ANTHONY TROLLOPE:
Barchester Towers

How might a timid bishop cope
With one so decadent as Slope,
Whose sweaty paws would paddle in
The palm of scrumptious Madeleine,
Or hardily aspire to hold
The chaster hand of Mrs Bold,
Which, when he ran the marriage race,
Slapped him right down to loser's place,
Leading the lucky Arabin
Herself (and Deanery) to win?
What crook could catch this straying sheep,

At once a bully and a creep,
Unscrupulous to pull the wool
Over the eyes of Quiverful,
His wolfish heart with ruth disguised
For Harding dehospitalised?
The conquest of the slippery Slope
Demands techniques of wider scope
Than those acquired by Proudie solo;
But his *Episcopari nolo*
Confirms his spouse, self-consecrated,
To be effectively translated,
And, should the flock attempt defiance,
Free to contract a fresh alliance
And stuff the unrepentant sinner
For the ensuing Sunday's dinner.
So Slope, a dainty joint to dish up,
Lamb basted by a female bishop
With bitter herbs and his own grease,
Slopes off, and Barchester's at peace.

MARY HOLTBY

ANTHONY TROLLOPE:
The Warden

Upon a rainy autumn eve,
When tracks lay deep in mire,
The bedesmen at the hospital
Sat dozing by the fire,
And told a stranger of the stir
That lately vex't all Barchester:

'John Bold, the surgeon 'twas,' quoth one,
'Who cried it were a shame
To rob us of our rightful dues –
The Bishop were to blame
For such a gross disparity
In doling Hiram's charity.

'That Warden Harding, he be paid
Eight hundred pound a year,
While all of us got scarce enough
For baccy and for beer –
They said it were a "sinecure",
Tho' what that be, I be not sure.

'Tom Towers of the "Jupiter",
He plied the lash so hard
That Warden Septimus, dear wight,
With mental stripes were scarred –
And felt such guilt upon him saddled,
The poor soul's wits were well-nigh addled.'

'But what good came of it at last?'
The stranger did inquire,
As Bunce the senior bedesman 'gan
To stoke the sinking fire.
'Are you now better fed and housed
Than ere this pother was aroused?'

'Why no!' they grieved. 'We too have cause
To count the scandal's cost.
Instead of gaining aught, we have
Our saintly Warden lost.
On t'other hand, it was, you see,
A famous Fleet Street victory.'

MARTIN FAGG

MARK TWAIN:
The Adventures of Huckleberry Finn

In lazy, ante-bellum days
A boy could spurn domestic ways
And drunken old Pap Finn's affrays
And head away down-river.

And on the raft, along with him,
Goes faithful, superstitious Jim,
Though some experience is grim,
Enough to make Huck shiver.

The king and duke, those men of guile,
Are good companions for a while,
But as for feuding – Southern-style –
It makes him want to vomit.

The river is a symbol (so
The critics say, and they should know);
Nobility *à la Rousseau*
Is what the kid learns from it.

Still, all good things come to an end,
And suddenly around a bend
Appear his old Missouri friend,
Tom Sawyer, and Aunt Polly.

Much sharper than a serpent's tooth
Is Huck's desire to stay uncouth.
What! 'Sivilise' a natural youth?
So he lights out, by golly.

BASIL RANSOME-DAVIES

JULES VERNE:
Around the World in Eighty Days

An Amah's Version

'Phileas Fogg b'long lich man. Go plentee time London Leform Club. Plentee man there. Likee too much betee. Lich man Fogg say he can lace lound world eighty days. "No can," say Club man. "Can do," say Fogg. "Me show. You pay?" "Okay," say Club peoples. Lich man then catchee Number One Flench boy. Talkee. "Jean Passepartout". He packee shirt, socks, toothblush. Buy tickets for steamer. Buy master map. Find fast steamer for India. Come monsoon. Big wind. All same typhoon. Number One Boy velly

seasick. Master Okay. India velly hot. Chow cully. India velly smelly.
Cully smelly. Number One boy belly sore. Master say "No can wait
more. Must go." Bombay plentee peoples. Parsee man die. Wife cly.
Why? She too die on pyre. Ai-yah. Big fire. Master see young widow
by fire. Aouda velly handsome. She cly. "I no wanchee die." "Come
quick," say Master. "We go." Aouda not slow. She lun chop-chop
and catchee tlain for Kholby with Master and Number One boy.
Kholby tlain finish. No more tlack. So Master catchee elephant for
Allahabad. All tlee lide topside in howdah. You wanchee me tellee
more? Okay. Master, Number One boy and Aouda closs water by big
steamer to Amelica. Big place Amelica. Too muchee snow. They lide
in sled. Many wolf makee chase. Master shoot wolf. *Boom. Boom.*
New York have got plentee ship. Must go chop-chop England, Master
paper say: "No can waste time." Bad Joss. Come London one day
too late. Master cly. Passepartout cly. Parsee lady cly. But now *biggee
mistake*. Master go lound world *east* to *west*. So he catchee *extla* day.
Club man must pay. Now Master Fogg *velly* happy. Aouda velly
happy. She mally master. Passepartout velly happy. He got ploper
job. No more tlavel.'

ARDA LACEY

VIRGIL:
The Aeneid

O wad the gods the giftie gi'e us
Bestowed by them on brave Aeneas,
Who staggered through unnumbered crises
While piggy-backing old Anchises,
And underwent extensive bathage
Before he landed up at Carthage.
He told his tale to Dido; found her
Most sympathetic, but the bounder
Left her to seek self-immolation,
Drawn on by his divine vocation.

The Ten Years War, the Trojan Horse,
He told her all about, of course,
But found it hard to get the lady's
Attention when they met in Hades.
However, as the time went by,
He soon had other fish to fry:
To settle permanent foundations
He needed amiable relations
With one whose daughter'd trothed her plight
To Turnus, whom he had to fight.
The outcome should bring no surprise:
His foe's respectable demise,
Marriage, the blueprint of a Rome
Destined to be a National Home –
A task involving wolves and twins:
But there another tale begins.

MARY HOLTBY

EVELYN WAUGH:
Brideshead Revisited

A fey alcoholic named Flyte,
Throws up on a carpet one night;
    Charles Ryder is charmed,
    To have his room balmed,
By a noble so stylishly tight.

Next day's invitation to dine,
On plovers' eggs, lobster and wine,
    Is raffishly bluff,
    Non-hetero stuff,
Where destinies darkly entwine.

But Sebastian's drinking won't stop
(Though Bridie hides every last drop);
    He rides with the hounds,
    Clutching Ryder's last pounds,
In pursuit of the grain and the hop.

How to Become Ridiculously Well-Read ...

In Tangier there's some expat self-pity,
With Kurt, a diseased Walter Mitty,
   Who's Germanically vain,
   Has the charm of a drain,
And *de rigueur* no funds for the kitty.

In England Charles smarts at the snub,
But, privately schooled, he won't blub;
   Instead woos the sister,
   To prove he's a mister,
But she prefers God, there's the rub.

TIM HOPKINS

H. G. WELLS:
The History of Mr Polly

Inefficient Mr Polly
Suffered much from melancholy,
Loathed his business and his wife,
Never seemed to fight for life;
Yet won a lady and her pub
Despite her brutal nephew's snub.

The story's moral's clear enough:
Even you can thrash a rough,
So if you feel your life's a flop
Leave your wife and burn your shop,
Paddle off and live in sin
With the owner of an inn.

PAUL GRIFFIN

H. G. WELLS:
Kipps

This is the story of Arthur Kipps,
Who found the truth about cups and lips.
From selling cloth in a draper's store
He came by a thousand a year and more.
The trouble started, as trouble may,
When he took some lessons from his fiancée
On the habits wealthy men display;
It broke his nerve, and he ran away.
'If only', he cried, 'I were back in trade!'
And he settled to marry a parlourmaid.
But still he thought his wealth ill-got
Till a crooked lawyer took the lot.
So back he went with a jump and hop
To his dear old life in a humble shop.
The Moral is short and rather snappy:
'Lawyers are there to make us happy.'

PAUL GRIFFIN

OSCAR WILDE:
The Importance of Being Earnest

Jack Worthing is free, fit and fine –
And he knows about women and wine.
　　Less coarse than a sandbag,
　　He was found in a *handbag* –
On the Brighton, that famous old line.

Algy Moncrieff does a Bunbury
To places like Paris or Sunbury –
　　To see a sick friend
　　Who is nearing his end –
But in truth he's at Joysville or Funbury!

There are two girls: Gwendolen, Cecily,
Who go round full of wit, and quite dressily.
　　Lady Bracknell's the Aunt –
　　Not her fault that it shan't
End in tears and in all ways quite messily!

C.'s governess, prune-faced Miss Prism,
Canon Chasuble; heresy, schism
    Fly away when *he's* there.
    She'd be willing to share
Any fate as his mate – cataclysm!

Now Jack's told one lie or another,
Told Cecily he has a brother
    Called Ernest – who's wicked –
    This isn't quite cricket
(No one knows yet who might be his mother).

So the Albany, country house lads
Must endure the girls' maidenly fads –
    C.'s a chick who in *her* nest
    Wants no one not Ernest.
Ditto Gwendolen. *Christen us cads!*

Is the favour they both of them ask.
It's the Canon's canonical task.
    But – one last catechism –
    Lady B. questions Prism,
And the Truth is revealed, with no mask!

That (how fateful and how well arranged!)
For a *novel* the young Jack was changed
    By Miss Prism, his nurse,
    And for better or worse
He's the brother of Alg., long estranged!

Even better, his true given name
Will revive the young Cecily's flame!
    For it's Ernest (no catch!),
    So it's game, set and match
(And the winner was wit in that game)!

GAVIN EWART

JOHN WYNDHAM:
The Day of the Triffids

A dazzlingly pretty comet shower
Causes universal blindness; in the wings
Lurks a hideous and evil-tempered flower
That strolls about and rattles as it stings.

A walking, talking veg.? It chills the spine!
(But also gives a novel way of glossing
That slightly surrealistic highway sign
Advising: CAUTION! HEAVY PLANT CROSSING)

The blinded population gets quite panicky;
There's lots of mayhem, pillage, rape and looting.
The triffids kill them off – they thrive on anarchy,
With their unbotanical approach to rooting.

The sighted hero (Bill) and girlfriend (Jo)
In a commune on the Downs (near Upper Beeding)
Make a bonfire of the triffids (see them glow!)
And devote themselves to years of happy breeding.

PETER NORMAN

NOTES ON CONTRIBUTORS

O. BANFIELD

Brought up in Wales. Educated at Swansea University. Came to London in 1941 to work in military intelligence and then married the journalist R. S. Pitt-Kethley. Has been a literary competition winner for many years.

page 42

REM BEL

Born in the year of Sputnik, in the swamps of the Waikato, New Zealand. Father sold butter-fat. Studied English Literature and Latin at Victoria University, Wellington; won a scholarship to do Scottish medieval studies at Edinburgh; chucked it in to work as a low-grade clerk, postcard seller at Edinburgh Castle, civil servant, DHSS claimant. At present working on an anti-nuclear-proliferation thriller. Likes real ale and cycling; dislikes travelling and writers who talk about their work.

pages 58, 170

W. S. BROWNLIE

Educated at Greenock Academy and Glasgow University. Rode in a tank with the Fife and Forfar Yeomanry from Normandy to the Baltic, but blew himself up before getting there. Awarded Military Cross. Enjoyed peacetime in the Ayrshire Yeomanry TA and wrote its history (*The Proud Trooper*, Collins, 1964) while trying to teach languages. Retired from school-teaching early, fleeing from educational theorists, in 1984. Enjoys scribbling.

pages 34, 114, 132

WENDY COPE

Born in Kent, in 1945. Read History at Oxford, and now lives in London. Taught in primary schools for some years and has also worked as a journalist. A selection of her poems appeared in *Poetry Introduction 5* (Faber and Faber, 1982).

pages 38, 62, 112

A. P. COX

Born in Alton, Hants, where he was educated at Eggar's Grammar School. Studied Aeronautical Engineering at University College (now University), Southampton, and during his working life in the Scientific Civil Service was responsible for a number of patented inventions. His work was terminated by a stroke in 1980, which fortunately did not affect his sense of humour and liking for juggling with words. Interests include music and the visual arts, particularly photography. He is a compulsive limerick writer, and was joint winner of the 1973 Daily Mail competition (since published in *The Art of the Limerick* by Cyril Bibby).

page 128

V. ERNEST COX
Born in 1944, a native of Wolverhampton, but now exiled in Welwyn Garden City. Works as Training Officer with Hertfordshire Youth and Community Service to support wife and two sons, and pay typewriter ribbon bills. Fanatical supporter of Wolverhampton Wanderers and other lost causes. Still wondering what he wants to be when he grows up.

pages 25, 29, 44, 45, 75, 86, 100, 103, 114, 122, 155, 170

GAVIN EWART
Born in 1916. Educated at Wellington College and Christ's College, Cambridge. Worked as a salesman, publisher, for the British Council, and in advertising as a copywriter. (Six years' war service, 1940–46). Now a free-lance writer.

page 178

JOE EWART
Collaborated on *Metamorphosis* when a sixteen-year-old student of Bill Greenwell's in 1976. Is now a graphic designer.

pages 105

MARTIN FAGG
Born in Kent. After Oxford taught in schools for twenty-five years in England, America and Australasia. His last teaching post was as Head of English at the Boys High School at Chichester, where he still lives. Now works as a full-time writer and reviewer. Main interests are history, music and Italy. Has been a regular literary competition winner since the 1950s.

pages 41, 55, 76, 93, 94, 96, 157, 172

BILL GREENWELL
Lives and works in Exeter. A regular contributor to the *New Statesman* and a number of other magazines. An inveterate weekend literary competitor. Aged thirty-one, he is married with one young son.

pages 53, 105, 133, 134

PAUL GRIFFIN

After being a Gurkha and a Chindit in the Second World War, spent three years at Cambridge, where he wrote poetry and contributed to pre-Muggeridge *Punch*. There followed a career of teaching English and running schools at home and abroad, which included a spell as a newsreader on Cyprus Radio under an assumed name. Retired early and released his literary energy, becoming a familiar figure in the weekly literary competitions.

pages 47, 48, 49, 58, 64, 65, 69, 83, 87, 90, 110, 118, 119, 139, 144, 162, 177, 178

MARY HOLTBY

Born in Cowley. Educated by her father's verse epistles, the Oxford English School, marriage, motherhood, occasional research and recurrent forays into teaching. Now resident in Chichester.

pages 18, 20, 23, 24, 57, 70, 82, 88, 90, 115, 126, 127, 134, 136, 143, 144, 147, 163, 171, 175

TIM HOPKINS

Born in Croydon, in 1943. Educated at East Barnet Grammar School and Newland Park College of Education. Has taught in both primary and secondary schools in England and Cyprus. Currently teaching in Luton. Has five children. Two teenage novels published. Hobbies include music and football.

pages 27, 59, 107, 113, 121, 140, 154, 155, 159, 165, 176

JOYCE JOHNSON

Educated at Tonbridge and Maidstone School of Art. After ten years in an advertising studio became free-lance illustrator of children's books. Entered first literary competition in 1940 and has done them on and off ever since. Now compiles crosswords for various national papers.

pages 21, 22, 24, 31, 33, 51, 55, 67, 102, 107, 108, 109, 116, 117, 141, 142, 145

ARDA LACEY

Journalist and poet. Contributor to the *Guardian*, the *Lady*, the *Daily Telegraph* and many other journals at home and abroad. Winner of the Julia Cairns Poetry Award, 1981. Work has appeared in numerous anthologies.

page 174

RUSSELL LUCAS

Born in Bombay in 1930. Is five sixteenths Scots, one quarter
Latvian, one eighth Welsh, one eighth African, one eighth
Eurasian, one sixteenth Armenian. Did National Service with East
Lancashire Regiment as a lance-corporal, 1948–9. Lifelong Labour
Party activist. Married, with two sons and a daughter. Lives in
Luton, where he is Banking and Foreign Exchange Manager of
US multi-national. For many years he was a frequent winner in
the *New Statesman* literary competition.

pages 68, 152

T.L.McCARTHY

Born in Glasgow, in 1917, and now lives in Barnes. A retired Customs
and Excise official. Produces verses and puzzles. His work has been
broadcast on the BBC, and has appeared in various magazines. His
verse crosswords and other puzzles appear regularly in the *Puzzler*.
London readers may have seen his Greater London Crossword in the
Londoner.

pages 46, 56, 66, 68, 120, 150, 151, 153, 164, 167

PETER NORMAN

Born in industrial Lancashire in 1951, but brought up in rural
Dorsetshire. Has a degree in English Literature (Nottingham) and
an MA in Applied Linguistics (London). Works as a lecturer in
English at a South London College of Further Education. Lives in
Brighton with his wife and two children. A regular literary
competition winner.

pages 26, 65, 73, 82, 112, 121, 180

PHYLLIS PARKER

Went from village school to Cambridge with the aid of various
scholarships. Took Arts degree, but found it was no gold-mine, so
worked as a secretary with writing as a sideline. Efforts to turn the
latter into her main line continue.

page 100

E.O.PARROTT

Born in London, in 1924. Educated at Grammar School, Shoreham-
by-Sea, and Brighton Technical College, where he took Honours
Degree in Geography. Wartime service as 'boffin' in Great Malvern.
Spent twenty years as a cartographer in the Admiralty Hydrographic
Dept, and fourteen years teaching General Studies at Havering
Technical College, while doing amateur drama and writing in spare
time. Married with one son, and lives on a narrow boat on the canals.

Now sets more literary competitions than he wins. Edited *The Penguin Book of Limericks* (Allen Lane, 1983) and *Limerick Delight* (Puffin, 1985).

pages 19, 39, 60, 137

FIONA PITT-KETHLEY

Born in 1954. Educated at the Chelsea School of Art. Has been writing full-time since 1978, supplemented by occasional work as a film extra and teaching. Published widely in the press, magazines and poetry anthologies. Has had three poetry collections published, including two in 1984 from Mammon and Marascat.

page 37

PASCO POLGLAZE

Retired civil servant. Aged but still bubbling. Writes in order to avoid being asked to mow the lawn, wash the dog or clean the car. Is therefore married, with one wife, two daughters, four grand-children and eight fairly sound teeth. Likes Beethoven, Benidorm and almond slices. A regular literary competitor.

pages 31, 63, 85, 92

BASIL RANSOME-DAVIES

A neurotic wartime baby and Dr Johnny Fever lookalike. A drop-out in the fifties, model husband and father in the sixties, romantic optimist in the seventies. Now teaches American Literature and Film Studies at a college in the West Midlands. Under a variety of pseudonyms has contributed to weekly literary competitions since the early seventies. Has published serious verse, reviews, fiction articles and a critical study of John Dos Passos. A Communist by conviction and an anarchist by temperament, his interests include drinking in French bars, the movies of Joseph von Sternberg and the unremitting pursuit of the bright elusive butterfly of love.

pages 35, 36, 74, 78, 83, 86, 99, 123, 125, 160, 161, 173

RON RUBIN

Born in Liverpool, in 1933, the fourth of six children. Educated at Liverpool College; dropped out of law school. Spent two years in RASC, and six years in family business. Has been a full-time musician since 1960 and has worked, toured, broadcast and recorded with many well-known jazz groups. At present solo pianist, largely on the Continent. Published in *The Penguin Book of Limericks* and *Limerick Delight*. Married with four children. Hobbies: Living.

pages 38, 44, 45, 52, 125, 135

STANLEY J. SHARPLESS

Born in 1910. Educated at Ilford County High School. First job was office boy in the advertising department of Kodak's. Later graduated to copywriter, and later became advertising manager. First appearance in print in the long-since defunct *Everyman Magazine* in 1932. Winner of *New Statesman* and other literary competitions for the last fifty years or so. Verse broadcast by BBC and appeared in many anthologies. Busier than ever in retirement, having at last discovered real *métier* as stand-up comic in Dorset village entertainments.

page 63

JOHN STANLEY SWEETMAN

Born in 1922, in Chertsey, Surrey, and educated at Basingstoke School and in the Royal Artillery. Briefly a publican, then spent thirty-three years at the fine end of the paper trade. Now retired and has been a regular literary competitor since 1973. A Catholic ecumaniac, he has six children and fourteen grandchildren, some of whom show literary promise.

page 77

ANNIE SYMONS

Collaborated on *Metamorphosis* when a sixteen-year-old student of Bill Greenwell's in 1976. Is now a textile designer.

page 105

PETER VEALE

Born in 1919. Told off by Head Prefect Edward Heath for being improperly dressed at Chatham House Grammar School, Ramsgate. Thirty years a Fleet Street sub-editor. Contributor to *That Was The Week That Was*. Member of team that produced a rare newspaper feature 'Tell Me If It Hurts' in the *Daily Herald* in the early 1960s. Once a regular winner in literary competitions.

pages 65, 111

CLAUDIO VITA-FINZI

Born in Sydney, Australia, in 1936. Educated in Argentina and the UK, now teaches at University College, London, and works on earthquakes. Realised he had an odd name when accused of having a pseudonym by a fellow competitor. Makes excellent cheesecake and is still trying to learn to play a saxophone he once bought for 10/-.

page 30

N.J.WARBURTON

Born in Woodford, in 1947. Educated there and at Leighton. Went
to teacher training college at Chichester. Lives in Cambridge.
Taught in primary schools for ten years. Writes plays, children's
books, etc.

BRENDA WHINCUP

Ex-nurse, ex-actress. Has had short stories on the 'Dial-a-Story'
service, but mostly writes poetry and gives readings. Work has
appeared in six Arts Council anthologies, and in many magazines.
Won gold medal at Cambridge Arts Festival. Was resident poet with
The Master Craftsman for four years. Work has also been anthologised
in the USA. Married, and now lives in Shropshire.

ACKNOWLEDGEMENTS

I would like to express my thanks to the following for help during the preparation of this book: Jonathan Barker of the Arts Council Poetry Library; Mike Woodward for technical assistance; Gaby Axtinat, for typing the final manuscript; and finally to Tricia, my wife, without whose help at all stages this book would never have seen the light of day.

The pieces on *King Lear* and *Macbeth* by Bill Greenwell were originally published in the Weekend Competition pages of the *New Statesman*. The pieces on *Richard III* and *Nicholas Nickleby* are new extended versions of verses which originally appeared in the *Spectator*. The piece on *The Importance of Being Earnest* by Gavin Ewart was first published in *The Young Pobble's Guide to His Toes*, Hutchinson, 1985.

READ MORE IN PENGUIN

In every corner of the world, on every subject under the sun, Penguin represents quality and variety – the very best in publishing today.

For complete information about books available from Penguin – including Puffins, Penguin Classics and Arkana – and how to order them, write to us at the appropriate address below. Please note that for copyright reasons the selection of books varies from country to country.

In the United Kingdom: Please write to *Dept. EP, Penguin Books Ltd, Bath Road, Harmondsworth, West Drayton, Middlesex UB7 ODA*

In the United States: Please write to *Consumer Sales, Penguin Putnam Inc., P.O. Box 999, Dept. 17109, Bergenfield, New Jersey 07621-0120.* VISA and MasterCard holders call 1-800-253-6476 to order Penguin titles

In Canada: Please write to *Penguin Books Canada Ltd, 10 Alcorn Avenue, Suite 300, Toronto, Ontario M4V 3B2*

In Australia: Please write to *Penguin Books Australia Ltd, P.O. Box 257, Ringwood, Victoria 3134*

In New Zealand: Please write to *Penguin Books (NZ) Ltd, Private Bag 102902, North Shore Mail Centre, Auckland 10*

In India: Please write to *Penguin Books India Pvt Ltd, 210 Chiranjiv Tower, 43 Nehru Place, New Delhi 110 019*

In the Netherlands: Please write to *Penguin Books Netherlands bv, Postbus 3507, NL-1001 AH Amsterdam*

In Germany: Please write to *Penguin Books Deutschland GmbH, Metzlerstrasse 26, 60594 Frankfurt am Main*

In Spain: Please write to *Penguin Books S. A., Bravo Murillo 19, 1° B, 28015 Madrid*

In Italy: Please write to *Penguin Italia s.r.l., Via Benedetto Croce 2, 20094 Corsico, Milano*

In France: Please write to *Penguin France, Le Carré Wilson, 62 rue Benjamin Baillaud, 31500 Toulouse*

In Japan: Please write to *Penguin Books Japan Ltd, Kaneko Building, 2-3-25 Koraku, Bunkyo-Ku, Tokyo 112*

In South Africa: Please write to *Penguin Books South Africa (Pty) Ltd, Private Bag X14, Parkview, 2122 Johannesburg*

BY THE SAME AUTHOR

Imitations of Immortality

A dazzling and witty selection of imitative verse and prose as immortal as the writers and works they seek to parody.

'Immensely funny . . . It will give pleasure not only to aficionados of the craft . . . but also to all lovers of literature who permit themselves a chuckle when their favourite writers have their legs pulled. It is a splendid book to read aloud from and to dip into and make one marvel at the comic inventiveness of pursuers of this most English genre' – *The Times Educational Supplement*

The Penguin Book of Limericks

'Wit, sharp comment, mood music, landscape, philosophy; all of these are in Mr Parrott's fine selection. Nor does it neglect the Double Limerick, the limeraiku, the Reverse Limerick or Beheaded Limericks, though sportiness, naughtiness and all the traditional qualities are well and tastefully represented, in several shades of blue . . .' – Gavin Ewart in the *Guardian*

'He seems to have read not only every previous collection but also far-flung limerick competitions, as well as being the recipient of many an improper verse from proud authors' – R. G. G. Price in *Punch*

How to be Tremendously Tuned In to Opera

Whether you are an opera buff or one of the *incognoscenti*, this delightful collection of parodies, satires and pastiches will inform and enlighten you about all aspects of the art form.

If you would like to become familiar with a large number of operas without the customary exertion or cost, this sparkling and witty anthology is just what the doctor ordered.

How to be Well-Versed in Poetry

E. O. Parrott and his team of tirelessly inventive contributors have produced wonderfully amusing examples of every trick, technique, rhyme, rhythm, syllable and stanza used in English verse. Unexpected delights include: The Pied Piper summed up in four lines, a little-known poetic gem by Ronald Reagan, a four-letter-word poem . . . and much, much more!